Father McBride's
TEEN
CATECHISM

*Based on the Catechism
of the Catholic Church*
ALFRED McBRIDE, O.PRAEM.

Nihil Obstat: Rev. John P. Bradley, S.T.L., M.A. (Oxon.)
                  Censor Deputatus
Imprimatur: William G. Curlin
                  Bishop of Charlotte
                  July 25, 1995

The nihil obstat and imprimatur are official declarations that a book or pamphlet is free of doctrinal or moral error. No implication is contained therein that those who have granted the nihil obstat and the imprimatur agree with the content, opinions or statements expressed.

Author's Acknowledgments
I would like to acknowledge the encouragement and support I received in writing this book from Father John Bradley, Mrs. Rose Bogan, Robert Gallagher, Fred Gallagher, Robert Lockwood and Greg Erlandson. I am most grateful for all they did to see this project come to fruition.

Acknowledgments
Jacquelyn Lindsey, Acquisitions Editor
Kelley Renz, Book Editor
Mary Machall, Editorial Assistant
Ron Mahannah, Layout and Design
Lewis Holland, Production

Excerpts from the English translation of the *Catechism of the Catholic Church* for the United States of America Copyright ©1994 United States Catholic Conference, Inc.—Libraria Editrice Vaticana. Used with permission. Scripture within the texts of the *Catechism of the Catholic Church* adapted from the *Revised Standard Version of the Bible*, ©1971 and the *New Revised Standard Version of the Bible*, ©1989 by the Division of Christian Education of the National Council of the Churches of Christ in the United States of America. All rights reserved. All other Scripture texts are taken from *The New American Bible With Revised New Testament*, ©1986 Confraternity of Christian Doctrine. All rights reserved.

ISBN: 0-87973-704-2

PRINTED IN THE UNITED STATES OF AMERICA

Cover design by Rebecca Heaston

Seton Media House would like to *Thank* the following patrons for providing this outstanding resource to the students of the Archdiocese of Washington D.C.

John T. Miller, Jr.
Sandy McMirtie
Donna F. Bethell
Louis J. Boland
W. Shepherdson Abell
Thomas J. Murray, CLU
Peter H. Planmondon, Sr.
Carl A. Ruppert
William J. Page
Commissioner John R. Simpson
Commissioner Edward F. Reilley, Jr.

Father McBride's
TEEN
CATECHISM

Washington D.C. Archdiocese

Table of Contents

Introduction

"How can they call on him in whom they have not believed? And how can they believe in him of whom they have not heard? And how can they hear without someone to preach?"

Romans 10:14

Millions of Catholics all over the world are buying the Catechism of the Catholic Church. Why? Because they want a sure guide for their faith. Because they are seeking a solid text to help them with their spiritual lives. Because they desire clarity and not confusion in their faith lives.

This new Catechism is a comprehensive, systematic and authoritative presentation of the truths of the Catholic Church. It is based on the revelation we have received from God in the Holy Scriptures and the

Apostolic Tradition and interpreted by our Spirit-guided Church in its Magisterium. It is filled with faith and inspires us to respond with faith to God's revelation of his plan of salvation accomplished in Jesus Christ.

Ultimately, the Catechism, on every page, calls us to faith in Jesus Christ, Son of God and Son of Mary, the God-man, Savior and Teacher and Example of the Christian life. It calls us to profess our faith as outlined in the Creed, to celebrate our faith in the Christian Mysteries—the sacraments, to live our faith through the Christian Moral Life expressed in Christ's laws of love, the beatitudes, the virtues and the ten commandments, to commit ourselves to a life of daily prayer, nourished by the Spirit especially through the seven petitions of the Our Father.

Another way of saying this is that the Catechism is divided into four pillars, each one of which draws us to a living, conscious and active faith in Jesus Christ:

I   The Creed .... The Faith Professed
II The Sacraments .... The Faith Celebrated
III Morality .... The Faith Lived
IV Prayer .... The Deepening of our Faith at All Levels

Though divided into these four parts, the pillars form a unity in the following ways: (1) The underlying theme is the divine plan of salvation in Jesus Christ. (2) The Holy Trinity embraces the entire book, with the Father shown as pouring out his blessings, the Son coming to redeem us, the Spirit abiding with us to teach and sanctify us. (3) Jesus is the center and life giving force of the whole text. (4) The dynamic of God revealing and our faith response to God is the dialogue of salvation present on every page.

The 803 pages of the English edition are both a challenge and graced opportunity for all Catholics. The text is a book of faith for us all. Nonetheless, it may seem daunting to some unless there is some guide available to unearth its riches. The purpose of this book is to open up the Catechism of the Catholic Church to our teen-age members. This book is not a substitute for the Catechism itself. But it is an introduction to the Catechism to help young readers acquire some sense of the meaning, the inner coherence and the direction the Catechism offers for becoming a knowledgeable, practicing and faith-filled young Catholic.

This book assumes that young people are only at the beginning of a lifelong faith journey, that they have many stages of faith growth ahead of them and that this is but one step in that enriching process. It also assumes that the readers will be led to explore the Catechism on their own, keep it at their bedsides and study desks for the rest of their lives, drawing from it the consoling and challenging message of Christ for their spiritual lives.

Along with the *Holy Scripture* and the celebration of the Sacraments, this Catechism should provide young people with a tool of Catholic learning as well as a guide to morality, prayer and the outline of a Catholic lifestyle.

How to Read and Study
this Guidebook

Each chapter contains the following elements:
1. Introductory faith story.
2. Question followed by three replies:
   A. A wrong or inadequate answer
   B. The response of the Catechism, a short explanation of the response, three questions followed by three answers taken from the Catechism.
   C. A reply to the material in answer (A) plus more response to the question.
3. A reflection on the topic, usually taken from the writings of a saint, theologian or outstanding Catholic.
4. *In My Life*—Three clusters of questions designed to help the readers apply the teaching to their personal lives.
5. Prayer
6. Glossary

The introductory faith story is often taken from a conversion experience, frequently autobiographical and always meant to be a mood setter for the reflection. It is a faith story because catechesis draws us to a living, conscious and active faith in Jesus.

The question has the advantage of awakening a sense of faith search in the reader. The first reply is always either wrong or inadequate. This method allows the text to introduce misunderstandings about Catholic teachings in a context of dialogue where the illumination of the truth can become more evident.

The second response to the question is always from the Catechism, thus serving several purposes. (1) It shows how the Catechism treats the teaching. (2) It offers the reader a sure norm for Catholic faith. (3) By the use of the three questions with answers taken from the Catechism, it helps the reader get into the Catechism itself, opens up the text and provides the sense of exploration of the Catechism intended by this guidebook.

The third response to the question follows up on the first one, correcting any remaining misunderstanding and presenting yet a few more thoughts on the teaching.

The reflection section quotes a variety of authors from the whole tradition of the Church and is designed to throw more light on the teaching. By quoting from such a wide fellowship of authors, this reflection provides the reader with a sense of historical continuity and community with the entire membership of our Catholic Tradition from Jesus and the apostles to the present.

The clusters of questions, *In My Life*, should enable the readers to apply the teaching to their personal lives, removing the exercise from being a purely abstract and academic study. Such an approach introduces the relevancy of the teaching as it arises from the challenges inherent in its call.

The prayer has two purposes, first to gather the readers in attentiveness to God and his gifts and graces. Second, it can be a prayer starter, going beyond the words in this text, each person invited to move more deeply into encounter with Christ.

Lastly, the glossary is simply one more way to tie in the teaching to one's life. Religious vocabulary is often technical, hence it needs definition for the sake of clarity, understanding and for a conversation where the participants know the key concepts in the discussion.

Jesus Christ is the Heart of all Catechesis

This guidebook was written in the spirit of Pope John Paul II's vision of catechesis (the teaching of religion), in which meeting Jesus and relating to him in faith is the purpose.

> "'At the heart of catechesis we find, in essence, a Person, the Person of Jesus of Nazareth, the only Son from the Father...who suffered and died for us and who now, after rising, is living with us forever.' To catechize is 'to reveal in the Person of Christ the whole of God's eternal design reaching fulfillment in that Person. It is to seek to understand the meaning of Christ's actions and words and of the signs worked by him.' Catechesis aims at putting 'people...in communion...with Jesus Christ: only he can lead us to the love of the Father in the Spirit and make us share in the life of the Holy Trinity.'"
>
> (Pope John Paul II,
> *On Catechesis, 5) Cf. Catechism, 426*

Chapter 1

The Desire for God
Is Written on Our Hearts

"I see that in every respect you are very religious."
—Acts 17:22

God Took Me By Surprise—
Rebellious, Wandering and Bored

"Following my easy shedding, at age 17, of what I thought was Christianity, I became over the next seven years of spiritual anarchy self centered, indulgent, impatient, concupiscent, and increasingly desperate — a perfect child of the 20th century.

But on the ship sailing home to America, I began seriously thinking of God, finally acknowledging the utter futility of trying to center my life around me. I admitted that I needed someone, something, other than myself to give purpose and meaning to my life. In short I needed God.

Once I uttered that prayer (although I did not realize it was a prayer) the rest came gradually. Logic drove me on. Did I believe there was a God who created the universe? Yes, because I did not believe the universe created itself. Did I believe that he had sent his Son to die for our sins and rise from the dead to give us everlasting life? Yes, because I did not believe that Christ was either a liar or a madman, but what he said he was, the Son of God. Did I believe the Bible was the divine word? Yes, because it came from the Father, Son and Holy Spirit. Were all churches the same, or was there one true church, or at least one true church for me? That, I decided, would require investigation." (Lee Edward's investigation led him to join the Catholic Church at age 26.)

Lee Edwards, Crisis Magazine, *January 1994, pages 20-21*

Are we naturally secular or essentially religious?

A. *Some say...*

Enlightenment thinkers of the 18th century paved the way for the idea of a purely secular man and woman. They invented deism which claimed God made the world and then left people in charge. The divine clockmaker wound up the clock and let it wind away on its own. In the minds of its adherents, this strategy removed God's influence from the world. Many took the next logical step and eliminated religion, faith and church from daily life. They argued that if God has nothing to do with life, why bother about religion? The Enlightenment had spoken and secular man was born.

Influential thinkers reinforced this view. Marx dismissed religion as the "opium of the people," —a drug, a religious chemical, whose addiction we should disavow. Freud said God is an illusion, a projection of the super-ego, our internal psychological policeman.

Scientific method, based on reason alone, excluded faith from its proceedings. History, poetry, literature and philosophy imitated the scientific method and gave us humanities without divinity. All these movements called themselves "modern."

We can find the results all around us. Films, novels, TV shows, opinion makers in newspapers and books celebrate secularity—a world without God. But they are not content to exile God, faith and religion. They mount political and propaganda campaigns to eradicate any religious influence —especially in area of moral values—in our schools, government and even our personal lives.

Karl Marx

B. *The Catechism Teaches...*

"Throughout history down to the present day, men have given expression to their quest for God in their religious beliefs and behavior: in their prayers, sacrifices, rituals, meditations, and so forth.

These forms of religious expression, despite the ambiguities they often bring with them, are so universal that one may well call man a *religious being."*
Catechism, 28

St. Augustine expressed this truth of our essential religious nature in the most famous of all his sayings "O God, you have made us for yourself and our hearts are restless until they rest in you." *(Confessions 1,1)*

Being fundamentally religious, we experience the drive to look for God. The material world and our own humanity open us to God.

Sigmund Freud

1. What do we learn from the material world about God?

"…starting from movement, becoming, contingency, and the world's order and beauty, one can come to a knowledge of God as the origin and the end of the universe." *Catechism, 32*

2. How is the human person drawn to God?

"…with his openness to truth and beauty, his sense of moral goodness, his freedom and the voice of his conscience, with his longings for the infinite and for happiness, man questions himself about God's existence. In all this he discerns signs of his spiritual soul. The soul, the 'seed of eternity we bear in ourselves, irreducible to the merely material,'[1] can have its origin only in God." *Catechism, 33*

3. Can we know God from reason?

"The Church, holds and teaches that God, the first principle and last end of all things, can be known …by the natural light of human reason.[2]" We have the ability to reason because we are created in God's image. Without reason, we could not accept God's self revelation. "In the historical conditions, in which he finds himself, however, man experiences many difficulties in coming to know God by the light of reason alone… This is why man stands in need of being enlightened by God's revelation…." *Catechism 36-38*

C. *As Catholics We Believe...*
Our faith teaches us that we are essentially religious, not merely secular. Enlightenment thinkers arbitrarily removed God's influence, presence and power from the world. To accept their opinion requires a secular act of faith.

- Marx's teachings, as expressed in various communist societies, have failed politically, economically and humanly. Religion is not the opium of the people. Religion is the vitamin of the soul.
- Many of Freud's theories have been shown to be far more of an illusion than the religion he dismissed.
- Scientific method today is being challenged today to include values and spiritual elements. It's one thing to make nuclear bombs and quite another to use them.
- The promises of secularism's "world without God" are not ministering to the deepest human hungers for spiritual, moral and religious values.

The fool says in his heart, "There is no God."

—Psalm 14:1

In My Life

1. What experiences have I had that help me believe in God's existence? Why is it that converts have so much stronger a sense of God's presence than I seem to have? How does my conviction about God's presence differ from when I was a child?

2. How would I like to see God's presence and influence be more evident in: my relationships, my music, my family, my school, the films, TV shows and magazines I encounter?

3. How would I try to convince a non-believer that God really exists? What would my prayer life and lifestyle contribute to persuading others about the truth of God's existence? How have others helped me to be certain and firm about God's presence and existence in my world and my life?

Prayer

Loving God, I thank you for the gift of creation in which I can see the traces of your existence. I praise you for my mind and heart whose restlessness leads me to you. In your love continue to bring me closer and closer to you.

Reflection

*Man has been rightfully described as a worshipping animal. If, for some reason he has no God, he will worship **something**. Common modern substitutes are the following: The state, success, efficiency, money, "glamor," power, even security. Nobody, of course, calls them God, but they have the influence and command the devotion which should belong to the real God. It is only when a man finds God that he is able to see how his worshipping instinct has been distorted and misdirected.*

J.B. Phillips, *Your God is Too Small,*
Macmillan, New York, 1961, page 58

Glossary

Enlightenment—An 18th century movement that espoused the primacy of reason and the exclusion of faith from intellectual endeavors.

Deism—A view of religion invented by Enlightenment thinkers. They claimed God made the world and left it to us. God was no longer involved with us as a loving, saving providential presence and power.

Chapter 2

Revelation:
God Calls Us
to Love and to Communion

"Love one another as I love you."
John 15:12

I am held so close to God
there is nothing in between.

"He showed me a little thing, the size of a hazelnut, in the palm of my hand, and it was round as a ball. I looked at it with my mind's eye and I thought, 'What can this be?' An answer came, 'It is all that is made.' I marveled that it could last, for I thought it might have crumbled to nothing it was so small. And the answer came into my mind, 'It lasts and ever shall because God loves it.' And all things have being because of the love of God.

In this little thing I saw three truths. The first is that God made it. The second is that God loves it. The third is that God looks after it.

What is he indeed that is maker and lover and keeper? I cannot find words to tell. For until I am one with him I can never have true rest nor peace. I can never know it until I am held so close to him there is nothing in between."

Mother Julian of Norwich, Enfolded In Love, *Darton Longman Todd, London, 1993, page 3*

(Mother Julian was a fourteenth century mystic who received 16 "showings" or revelations from God. She counseled many people with holy wisdom. The first woman to write a book in English, her writings have brought countless numbers of people to faith in God.)

Is revelation necessary?

A. *Some say...*
Since the Church teaches that we can come to know God by the light of reason, it would seem that revelation is not necessary. St. Paul says that we can know God from conscientiously examining the world. "Ever since the creation of the world, his invisible attributes of eternal power and divinity have been able to be understood and perceived in what he has made." *(Romans 1:20)*

In the Old Testament, King David taught the same truth. "The heavens declare the glory of God and the firmament proclaims his handiwork. Day pours out the word to day and night imparts knowledge. Through all the earth their voice resounds." *(Psalm 18:2,5)* In other words, God speaks of his presence and existence in the wonders of creation.

Therefore, when we apply the light of our minds to creation we can infer the reality of God. Hence it would seem there is no need for a revelation to know God. We can figure it out on our own.

B. *The Catechism Teaches...*
The Catechism teaches that revelation was necessary. "In the historical conditions in which he finds himself, however, man experiences many difficulties in coming to know God by the light of reason alone... This is why man stands in need of being enlightened by God's revelation...about those things that exceed his understanding." *Catechism 37,38*

By itself, our reason finds it hard to believe in God. Why? Because our sensuality, fantasy in our imaginations, weakness in our wills and disorder in our desires—the consequences of original sin—cloud our minds. Our disruptive passions distract us from knowing God. Revelation counters this by giving us a certain, clean vision of God, free from error.

Revelation also tells us truths about God which are beyond the light of reason. Revelation unfolds for us the love God has for us and the compassionate divine plan of salvation. Revelation discloses God's inner life in the Trinity, the truths about the Son of God becoming a man to save us, the graces of the Church and the Sacraments and our adoption by God as his sons and daughters. Reason could never know any of these truths on its own. We needed revelation for this.

God accomplished this revelation gradually in a series of covenants: first with our first parents, then with all mankind through Noah, then with Abraham, Moses and the prophets and finally, in its fullness in Jesus Christ.

1. Why is there Revelation?

"It pleased God, in his goodness and wisdom, to reveal himself and to make known the mystery of his will. His will was that men should have access to the Father, through Christ, the Word made flesh, in the Holy Spirit, and thus become sharers in the divine nature."[3] *Catechism, 51*

2. Will there be any new Revelation?

"The Christian economy, ... since it is the new and definitive Covenant, it will never pass away; and no new public revelation is to be expected before the glorious manifestation of our Lord Jesus Christ."[4] *Catechism, 66*

3. What about "private" revelations?

"Throughout the ages, there have been so-called 'private' revelations, some of which have been recognized by the authority of the Church. They do not belong, however, to the deposit of faith. It is not their role to improve or complete Christ's definitive Revelation, but to help live more fully by it in a certain period of history." *Catechism, 67*

As Catholics We Believe...

The light of reason can only tell us that God exists and is present to our world. We also need revelation to know how much God loves us and all the truths of salvation from sin that flow from that love. To recognize revelation, we need the light of faith. This is our response to revelation and will be the topic of our next lesson.

The supreme example of revelation is Jesus Christ. Because God is so profound a mystery, our words about him always fall short of his reality. In Jesus Christ, God has made visible his inner mystery.

Revelation is a source of both humility and joy. Humility, in that we realize that our reason alone cannot reach all that can be known about God. Joy, in that God lovingly shares his inner life and hidden plans of saving affection with us. God honors us with the gift of reason. Further, God provides us with possibilities of personal happiness and fulfillment that we had not imagined until he made it known to us.

Reflection

"Once he has given us his Son, who is his Word, God has no other word to give us. He has said everything to us, all summed up in that unique Word. What he said partially in the prophets, he has said entirely in his Son."

St. John of the Cross,
Ascent of Mount Carmel, Book II. Chapter 20

"I am the light of the world."

John 8:12

After the great flood, God made a covenant with Noah, and set the rainbow and the clouds as a symbol of the divine promise that never again would the waters of a flood destroy the earth. Noah trusted God's Revelation because of his faith.

In My Life

1. "The saints in heaven turn their will away from everything, except what God would have them know. This should be our will too." (*Mother Julian of Norwich*, Ibid. p. 15) What must I do to become more like the saints? What prevents me from turning myself to God? God wants to hold me so close that there is nothing in between. What stands between me and God?

2. Picture the scene in the story of the Prodigal Son where the father hugs his son and calls for a celebration. All walls have fallen between parent and offspring. How would I feel, whether I am a son or a daughter, in receiving such forgiving love from a parent? Suppose I am receiving it from God. What are three reactions I might have?

3. How do I recognize the kindness of God in the gift of revelation? Which image of Jesus best reveals the meaning of God for me? How would I best express my gratitude to God for the gift of revelation?

Prayer

O God, our journey to you is in three stages. By the light of reason we behold your presence and existence. By the light of faith we encounter the revelation of your inner life and the divine plan of salvation. By the light of glory, we will one day, with your grace, enjoy you face to face. We praise you for these gifts and pray that we may walk toward you with joy in the companionship of Jesus Christ and the power of the Spirit.

Glossary

Revelation—The acts in history whereby God told us both about the inner life of the Holy Trinity and the Trinity's desire to express love for us by (1) a divine plan of salvation from sin (2) a divine, loving desire to bring us happiness (3) the fulfillment of this in Jesus Christ the Church and the Sacraments.

Covenant—The acts of love and union whereby God revealed the divine plan of salvation to us.

Chapter 3

Faith:
My Response to God's Revelation

"Love one another as I love you."
John 15:12

His Whole Body
Strained Upward With Joy

Nagasaki, Japan, February 6, 1597.

The crosses were set in place. Paul Miki saw himself standing in

the noblest pulpit he had ever filled. He was dying for the Gospel he preached. "As I come to this supreme moment of my life, I am sure none of you would suppose I want to deceive you. And so I tell you plainly: there is no way to be saved except the Christian way. My religion teaches me to pardon my enemies and all who have offended me. I do gladly pardon the emperor and all who have sought my death. I beg them to seek baptism and become Christians themselves."

Then he looked at his comrades and began to encourage them in their final struggle. Joy glowed in all their faces, and in Louis' most of all. When a Christian cried out to him that he would soon be in heaven, his whole body strained upward with such joy that every eye was fixed on him.

Then according to Japanese custom, the four executioners began to unsheathe their spears. At this dreadful sight, all the Christians cried out "Jesus, Mary!" And the storm of anguished weeping then rose to batter the very skies. The executioners killed them one by one. One thrust of the spear, then a second blow. It was over in a very short time.

From an account of the martyrdom of St. Paul Miki
and his companions, by a contemporary writer.
Liturgy of the Hours, *Volume II,*
Catholic Book Publishing, New York, 1976, Pages 1664-5

Is faith a surrender to a person or a belief in a doctrine?

A. *Some say...*

The vivid account of the martyrdom of St. Paul Miki and his companions, which we just read, clearly demonstrates that faith is an act of surrender to the person of Jesus Christ. We die for those we believe in and trust. Faith is always a very personal matter.

Even the first line of the Creed reflects the personal quality of faith. We say, "I believe in God." Religious writings are filled with faith in terms of relationship language. Convert stories, accounts of religious experiences and reports of courageous moral behavior center on the personal aspect of faith. People speak of intimacy with Jesus as the reason why they became Catholics. Martyrs testify that the personal presence of the Spirit gave backbone to their faith.

With these and many other similar arguments and examples, it seems clear that faith is only a personal surrender to God, Father, Son and Spirit. It is not belief in a doctrine.

B. *The Catechism Teaches...*

...that faith is: (1) a personal commitment to God; (2) an intellectual assent to the truths and doctrines of revelation; (3) and the reason for spiritual and moral behavior.

Faith is not an either-or action. Faith embraces both belief in the person of Jesus and belief in the message of Jesus. Jesus clearly related warmly and personally to those he met. Jesus also taught truths that he wanted them to believe. He said, "I am the truth." He could also say, "I have the truth." Witness is important. So also is doctrine. The person gives life to the message. The message deepens our relationship with the person Both are essential. I believe in Jesus. I also believe in what Jesus teaches.

1. What is faith?

Faith is both a personal commitment to God on the part of a human being and a "free assent to the whole truth that God has revealed." Faith is a gift from God, a supernatural virtue infused by him. Faith is an authentically human act. "Believing is an act of the intellect assenting to the divine truth by command of the will moved by God through grace."[5] *Catechism, 150, 154, 155*

2. Why is faith connected to obedience?

"To obey (from the Latin *ob-audire*, to 'hear or listen to') in faith is to submit freely to the word that has been heard, because its truth is guaranteed by God, who is Truth itself. Abraham is the model of such obedience offered us by Sacred Scripture. The Virgin Mary is its most perfect embodiment." *Catechism, 144*

3. Why say "We Believe" as well as "I Believe"?

"Faith is a personal act.... But faith is not an isolated act. No one can believe alone, just as no one can live alone.... I cannot believe without being carried by the faith of others, and by my faith I help support others in the faith.

"'I believe' (*Apostles' Creed*) is the faith of the Church professed personally by each believer, principally during Baptism. 'We believe' (*Niceno-Constantinopolitan Creed*) is the faith of the Church confessed by... the liturgical assembly of believers." *Catechism, 166-7*

C. *As Catholics We Believe...*

In faith we respond to God the revealer. God says, "I love you and want to save you from your sins and bring you happiness. Will you accept me?" Our faith moves us to reply, "Yes, Lord. Thank you for the gift of yourself." But God also reveals a message to help us live out salvation. "Will you accept and obey my truths of love that will make you free and happy?" Faith should move us to accept the message too. "Yes, Lord, I believe what you tell me because you are truth-full." Hence it is a mistake to ignore either the person or message of God in matters of revelation and faith response.

Reflection

*I seek not, O Lord, to search out your depth, but I desire in some measure to understand your truth, which my heart believes and loves. Nor do I seek to understand that I may believe, **but I believe that I may understand**. For this too I believe that **unless I first believe, I shall not understand**.*

On the one hand, right reason requires that we believe the deep things of the Christian religion before presuming to subject them to the analysis and test of reason.

On the other hand, it looks to me like indolent neglect if, already established in the faith, we do not take the trouble to gain an intellectual intimacy with what we believe.

St. Anselm of Canterbury
Quoted from English Spirituality *by Martin Thornton, Cowley, Cambridge, MA 1986 pages 158-9*

"I believe that I may understand."

St. Anselm

In My Life

1. Among human beings, who am I most likely to believe, a liar or an honest person? Why is it most sensible of all to believe in God? Why is it important to believe both in God in a personal way and in the truths, doctrines and messages God has revealed?

2. Read again the quote from St. Anselm. Why do you think he begins with faith and then goes to understanding? Isn't it more practical to start with understanding and then go to belief? In other words, how can there be understanding of something that is not yet believed? How does Anselm's teaching apply to this religion study that you are involved in?

3. The Catechism speaks of the "obedience of faith." Obedience means hearing and obeying. Why is faith an act of obedience? What would such faith obedience mean for your moral life? Why do we say that faith is a loving response to God's loving revelation?

Prayer

Dear God, I think today of Abraham. You asked him to leave his home and friends and take his family to a strange land and start a new life. You promised to make him the father of a new people. He obeyed you and became our father in faith.

I think also of Mary at the Annunciation. You asked her to become the mother of your divine Son through the power of the Holy Spirit. She obeyed your invitation in this and every other call you asked of her throughout her life. She obeyed you and became our mother in faith.

Abraham modeled faith. Mary both modeled it and perfectly

fulfilled what faith should be. I ask the grace of faith that will make me both like Abraham and Mary in my faith life. I beg this through Jesus in the power of the Spirit. Amen.

Abraham

Glossary

Faith—A gift from God that enables me both to have a personal relationship with the Holy Trinity as well as the capacity to believe in revelation—the truths of salvation from sin and the path to happiness and love.

Creeds—The Apostles' Creed is an early baptismal Creed that authentically reflects the faith of the Apostles. The Nicene Creed, recited at Mass, is the Creed of Councils of Nicea (325) and First Constantinople (381).

Chapter 4

Revelation Is Communicated Through Tradition and Scripture

"I handed on to you as of first importance what I also received..."
I Cor 15:3

On Becoming a Catholic, the Abbot Said, "It Must Be for Always."

Msgr. Ronald Knox

At no time in my life have I desired anything else in the way of religion other than membership in the body of people which Jesus Christ left to succeed him. Until the age of fifteen I believed in the Blessed Trinity, the Incarnation, the Life, Death, Resurrection and Ascension of our Savior, Heaven, Hell, and the forgiveness of our sins, only through the atoning merits of the Precious Blood.

I have never ceased to believe in these things, though later I experienced temptations against the Faith, and found my way to the combatting of them.

At Eton, I learned to value other doctrines besides—the idea of a continuous ministry unifying Church history. I learned to think of Church traditions as possessing a special claim on the Church's obedience. At Oxford, I learned more definitely to attach a miraculous efficacy to the Eucharist and to approach and ask the aid of God's saints, to assert the endowment of his Mother, to think of the Bishops of Rome as the successors of St. Peter. Later, I came to regard the Bishop of Rome, not merely as the Primate, but the natural administrative head and doctrinal teacher of Christians. I have never ceased to believe in these things.

(On his retreat at Farnborough Abbey, preparing for entry into the Catholic Church, Ronald Knox heard the abbot say to him, "It must be for always.")

Msgr. Ronald Knox, A Spiritual Aeneid, Sheed and Ward,
New York, 1958, Pages 211-213

Is the Bible alone the sole source of God's revelation?

A. *Some say...*
Since we call the Bible the Word of God, it is evident that it is the sole source of divine revelation. Considering the extraordinary reverence we give to Scripture, the place of honor it has in all our churches, one cannot argue otherwise. Church councils at Hippo (393) and Carthage (397 and 419) solemnly declared that the books which now compose our Bible were truly God's Word and divine revelation.

The Protestant reformers of the 16th century—Luther and Calvin—emphasized the incredible value of Scripture as the true and only fountain of divine revelation. Saints and holy people throughout all of Christian history tell us how deeply their faith was nourished by the Bible. St. Jerome claimed that "Ignorance of Scripture was ignorance of Christ." Here indeed is the sacred source of revelation.

But in our own time some have spoken of *continuous revelation,* as though some new revelation is being given. This contradicts the teaching of the Catholic Church which teaches that in Jesus Christ, his person, life, message and saving deeds, revelation has been completed. *Catechism, 66* The Bible alone contains this revelation and these new theories are to be rejected.

B. *The Catechism Teaches...*
...that revelation is communicated both in tradition and scripture.
"Sacred Tradition and Sacred Scripture, then, are bound closely together and communicate one with the other. For both of them, flowing out from the same divine well-spring, come together in some fashion to form one thing and more towards the same goal."[6] *Catechism, 80*

Jesus Christ called the apostles, trained them in his meaning and message and commanded them to preach the Gospel. In the beginning, the apostles preached the Gospel orally, witnessed it by their example and in the institutions they established under the guidance of the Holy Spirit.

Gradually they, and others associated with them, committed the Gospel to writing under the inspiration of the same Holy Spirit.

To make sure the living Gospel should always be preached and witnessed until the end of time, the apostles left us bishops as their successors with their own teaching authority. This is the theme of mission. The Father sent the Son. The Son sent the apostles. The apostles sent the bishops. The Holy Spirit leads, guides, teaches and protects the bishops so they truly and in a living manner communicate Christ's Gospel entrusted to the apostles and their successors.

The one fountain of revelation, embodied and fulfilled by Jesus Christ, flows into two intimately connected streams: The Living Tradition of the Church and the Living Word of Sacred Scripture.

1. What is Tradition?

"This living transmission, accomplished in the Holy Spirit, is called Tradition, since it is distinct from Sacred Scripture, though closely connected to it. Through Tradition, 'the Church, in her doctrine, life and worship perpetuates and transmits to every generation all that she herself is, all that she believes.'" *Catechism, 78*

2. What are the two ways revelation is communicated?

"'*Sacred Scripture* is the speech of God as it is put down in writing under the breath of the Holy Spirit.'[8]

"'And [Holy] *Tradition* transmits in its entirety the Word of God once which has been entrusted to the apostles by Christ the Lord and the Holy Spirit. It transmits it to the successors of the apostles.... Both Scripture and Tradition must be accepted and honored with equal sentiments of devotion and reverence.'[9]" *Catechism, 81-82*

3. What are the criteria for interpreting Scripture?

a. *"Be especially attentive 'to the content and unity of the whole Scripture.'[10]"*

b. *"Read the Scripture within the 'living Tradition of the whole Church.'[11]"*

c. *"Be attentive to the analogy of faith.[12]* By 'analogy of faith,' we mean the coherence of the truths of faith among themselves and within the whole plan of Revelation." *Catechism, 112-14*

C. As Catholics We Believe...

Church history demonstrates repeated attempts to drive a wedge between Scripture and Tradition. Reformers often like to pit the "pure doctrine of Scripture" against the "sins and corruption of the Church." We cannot deny the sinfulness of Church members. We also strongly affirm the sanctity of countless members of the Church throughout history, above all, the unmatched holiness of the Virgin Mary, our Blessed Mother, preserved from original sin and supreme witness of faith.

We further argue that the Holy Spirit abides with the Church to maintain the faith of the Church and her mission to pass on the authentic Gospel of Christ to each generation By the will of Christ and the work of the Spirit, the Magisterium of the Church (her teaching office as embodied in the pope and bishops) both created the Sacred Scripture and provides a true and trustworthy interpretation of what it means for our salvation from sin, present happiness and future glory.

Therefore, we do not, as Catholics, believe that revelation is in the Scripture alone, but it is also in Sacred Tradition as manifested in the living Church, the Body of Christ.

Reflection

The French writer Paul Claudel compared the Church's Tradition to walking, with one foot on the ground and the other in the air. If we keep both feet on the ground, we do not budge. If we have both feet in the air, we are foolhardy and lose our bearing. Tradition has an enduring element. It is rooted in the apostolic preaching and an openness to change, moving forward through time under the guidance of the Spirit.

J. Michael Miller, C.S.B.
Life's Greatest Grace. Why I Belong to the Catholic Church,
OSV, Huntington, IN, 1993 Page 42

𝕴𝕟 𝕸𝖞 𝕷𝖎𝖋𝖊

1. Visualize Pentecost morning. Read Acts 2. See the Upper Room. Mary is there with the 12 apostles and 120 disciples. They are finishing nine days of prayer for the coming of the Spirit. Then their prayers are answered. The Spirit comes in wind and fire. Filled with the Spirit, the apostles and disciples flow into the square outside and Peter preaches the first sermon of the Church making numerous converts. What does the scene tell you about revelation? Is there a written New Testament yet? Is there a living Church Tradition?

2. Think of examples of schools, businesses and sports teams. They all have written authoritative records. They also have bosses, coaches and principals. How does this same setup appear in the communication of revelation?

3. Read again Msgr. Knox's account of his conversion. What does he state about his belief in Tradition? What might you see of yourself in his story?

Mary, with the twelve Apostles on Pentecost morning

"Timothy, guard what has been entrusted to you."

I Timothy, 6:20

Prayer

Holy Spirit, you oversee with your divine warmth the communication of revelation to the prophets and apostles. Through them and their associates you bring about the Sacred Scripture and Sacred Tradition, both flowing from the one fountain of your revelation. I pray for faith in the life giving forces of revelation found in these two expressions. Amen.

Chapter 5

I Believe in God the Father Almighty

"Holy, holy, holy is the Lord of hosts!"
Isaiah 6:3

I Heard the Voice of God

"This is how it happened," she told me. "I was traveling to Darjeeling by train, when I heard the voice of God." When I asked her how she had heard this voice above the noise of a rattling train, she replied with a smile, "I was sure it was God's voice. I was certain that he was calling me. The message was clear: I must leave the convent to help the poor by living among them. This was a command, something to be done, something definite. I knew where I had to be. But I did not know how to get there."

As she spoke, her face glowed with happiness, peace and assurance. I wondered: was it a vision or an inspiration? Did she hear a voice—or something else? In view of what else was going on, how could she be sure?

She broke into my thoughts. "The form of the call is neither here nor there. It was something between God and me. What matters is that God calls each of us in a different way. It is no credit to us that he does so. What matters is that we should answer the call! In those difficult, dramatic days I was certain that this was God's doing and not mine, and I am still certain. And, as it *was* the work of God I knew that the world would benefit from it."

And so it has been. I think of Elizabeth's words to Mary: "Blessed are you who believed that what was spoken to you by the Lord was fulfilled." *(Luke 1:45)*

Mother Teresa, the Early Years
by David Porter, Eerdmans,
Grand Rapids, 1986 Page 56

Is God personal or impersonal?

A. *Some say...*
It would seem that God is impersonal. The nature religions of ancient times viewed God as an impersonal power. Babylonians worshipped the moon. Egyptians adored the sun. Fertility cults imagined rain as the male god and earth as the female goddess. They reflected this in sexual sculptures. Some revered serpents or bulls. Their gods were borrowed from the impersonal world of the cosmos or animals.

Much public discussion of God today is still in non-personal terms. The film "Star Wars" has the sage saying, "The force be with you." Critics of Christianity have claimed that even Christians do not deal with God personally, but rather as a vague power "up there" beyond human affairs and not involved here. Whereas the ancients particularized their gods in nature images, the moderns generalize God as a kind of space age radar. Advocates of New Age spirituality carry this to its logical extreme, making all of us "part of God."

All who argue that God is impersonal choose some type of created being as God. The Druids thought big trees in dark grottoes were gods. New Agers simply believe all of us are God.

These views result in many gods or polytheism. If this enduring way of thinking of God be true, then God is impersonal.

B. *The Catechism Teaches...*
...that God is personal, One, Loving. With our reason we could come to know the existence and presence of God. But we need revelation to experience God as personal This is exactly what happened to Moses at the burning bush. Moses asked God his name. God replied, "I AM..."
(Exodus 3:14)

God reveals that he is not a vague, impersonal force, not a tree or a star or a bull—or even the sum total of all humans. God is an "I" to whom we need to reply in a personal encounter. The powerful "I" of God speaks to the "thou" in each of us, inviting us to accept love, mercy, salvation and happiness.

At the same time, the "I AM" is a divine mystery. In Scripture, a mystery is both light and hiddeness. The fire of the burning bush brought to Moses the light and visibility of a personal God. The fact that Moses needed to take off his shoes and bury his head in adoration signified the hiddeness, that is, the depth of God that is yet to be known. God reveals something of himself and conceals his immensity which can only be taken in by us a little at a time. Yes, the "I AM" is very personal.

1. What does it mean to speak of the "One" God?

"To Israel, his chosen, God revealed himself as the only One: 'Hear, O Israel: The LORD our God is one LORD; and you shall love the LORD your God with all your heart, and with all your soul, and with all your might.'[13] Through the prophets, God calls Israel and all nations to turn to him, the one and only God." *Catechism, 201*

2. Who revealed God as Father?

"Jesus revealed that God is Father in an unheard of sense: he is Father not only in being Creator; he is eternally Father by his relationship to his only Son who, reciprocally, is Son only in relation to his Father. 'No one knows the Son except the Father, and no one knows the Father except the Son and anyone to whom the Son chooses to reveal him.'[14]" *Catechism, 240*

3. What is the connection between love and God?

St. John affirms that "God *is* love." *(I Jn 4:8, 16; italics mine)* God's very being is love. By sending his only Son and the Spirit of love in the fullness of time, God has revealed to us his most intimate secret: God *is* an eternal exchange of love, Father, Son and Holy Spirit, and has destined us to share in that exchange.
See Catechism, 733

C. *As Catholics We Believe...*

We reject all impersonal presentations of God, whether as an animal, a tree, a mountain or some star or planet, let alone a shadowy cosmic force or merely the extension of ourselves. When the real, personal, God of love and mercy is denied or ignored, then substitutes will appear. Today we see the re-appearance of satanic cults, reverence for crystals, witchery and goddess worship. In all of these movements God is reduced to an impersonal reality which humans invent and identify with the subhuman world, or even humans themselves.

Revelation wholesomely corrects this aberration by sharing with us the real God who loves and cares for us and calls us to a life of faith, love and responsibility—and ultimately to absolute joy and happiness.

Reflection

I believe we must render most reverent homage to him who created us and stilled the sea and told the winds to be calm and multiplied the loaves and fishes. He is transcendent and He is imminent. He is closer than the air we breathe and just as vital to us. I speak impetuously, from my heart, and if I err theologically in my expression, I beg forgiveness.

Dorothy Day, *Meditations*, Newman Press, New York, 1970 Page 73

Mother Teresa

In My Life

When I compare Mother Teresa's experience of God's call with that of Moses, what are the similarities? The differences? In my own experience of God what elements from the story of Mother Teresa and Moses might apply in life? How strongly do I hear God calling me as he called them?

2. As I read the argument about whether God is Personal or impersonal, what are times in my life when God seems impersonal to me and moments when he appears very personal? How can I come to a deeply personal relationship with God?

3. Scripture teaches me that God is mystery, both revealing himself to me and yet hidden, meaning God has much more love to share with me. In a much lesser sense I am a mystery. How does that show up in my relations with others? If God is love, what effect will that have on my relationship with him?

"Thus have I gazed toward you in the sanctuary to see your... glory..."

Psalm 63:3

Prayer

Holy God, I praise your name. Lord of all, I bow before you. All on earth do praise your name. All in heaven above adore you. I revere your mystery and rejoice in your boundless love for me. You are my one and only God. To you alone be glory.

Glossary

Transcendent—To be above or beyond. Applied to God this means he is above and beyond all that is created.

Imminent—To be "right here." Applied to God this means that he wills to dwell among us in Christ and the Spirit, to be involved with us to love and save us.

Divine Mystery—Refers to the double aspect of God who gradually makes himself known to us, but who also is hidden, an immense Love that is yet to be known.

Chapter 6

The Holy Trinity: Glory to the Father, Son and Spirit

"He saw the Spirit of God descending like a dove [and] coming upon him. And a voice came from the heavens, saying, 'This is my beloved Son, with whom I am well pleased.'"

Matthew 3:16-17

You Called. You Cried Aloud to Me. You Touched Me.

Under your guidance I entered into the depths of my soul because your aid befriended me. I saw the light that never changes casting its rays over my mind. Your light shone upon me in its brilliance. I thrilled with love and dread alike. I heard your voice calling from on high, "I am the food of full-grown men... I am the God who IS." I heard your voice as we hear voices that speak to our hearts.

Late have I learned to love you, Beauty at once so ancient and so new! You were within me, and I was in the world outside myself. You were within me, but I was not with you. The beautiful things of this world kept me far from you and yet, if they had not been in you they would have no being at all.

You called me. You cried aloud to me. You broke my barrier of deafness. You shone upon me. Your radiance enveloped me. You put my blindness to flight. You shed your fragrance about me. I drew breath and now I gasp for your sweet fragrance. I tasted you and now I hunger and thirst for you.

You touched me and I am inflamed with love of your peace.

St. Augustine, *Confessions*, Books VII, 10; X, 27; Penguin Books, London, 1961, Pages 146-7; 231-2

Is faith a surrender to a person or a belief in a doctrine?

A. *Some say...*

We saw in our last lesson that the Catechism *(201)* and Scripture *(Dt. 6:4-5)* both assert the oneness of God. There can only be one God. This remains the constant teaching of two of the world's great religions, Judaism and Islam. The doctrine of the Trinity seems to be a departure from this revealed truth. Moreover, the term Trinity does not appear in the Bible.

Faced with this question, several fourth century thinkers proposed solutions to maintain the oneness of God. A Lybian-born priest, Arius, preached that Jesus was not divine in the same sense the One God was divine. He argued that God created a Logos, a Word, by which he made the world. When the world needed salvation, this Word became flesh in Jesus. After Good Friday, God rewarded the Word-Jesus with resurrection and adopted him as a "minor divinity."

Later, an archbishop of Constantinople, Nestorius, said that no human mother (Mary) could be a mother of God. Mary simply gave birth to a human Jesus, who later acquired some kind of divinity.

Today many teach only the humanity of Jesus, emphasizing his wonderful example and beautiful teachings about love. This reflects the conviction that God is one and not triune.

Saint Augustine

B. *The Catechism Teaches...*

"The mystery of the Most Holy Trinity," One God in three divine persons, "is the central mystery of Christian faith and life." It is the mystery of God in himself. It is therefore the source of all the other mysteries of faith...." *Catechism, 234*

Scripture indeed professes that God is one. But Scripture also speaks of God as Father, Son and Spirit. Already in the Old Testament, the People of God were calling him Father. God is called Father 170 times in the gospels.

Secondly, Jesus is frequently called the Son of God in the New Testament. At the Baptism and the Transfiguration, the voice from heaven says, "This is my Son." Mark's gospel begins with, "The beginning of the gospel of Jesus Christ [the Son of God]." *(Mk 1:1)* Toward the end of this gospel, the Centurion says, "Truly this man was the Son of God!" *(Mk 15:39)* Jesus talks to and about God as his Father, even using the intimate family term, "abba"—the equivalent of daddy or papa. There are numerous other scriptural references for Christ's divine sonship. (See *John 1* and *Phillipians 2.)*

Thirdly, the Spirit is often spoken of as a divine person. Jesus tells the apostles that both he and the Father will send the Spirit to teach them the truth, remind them of it and protect them in it. *(Jn 14:17,26; 16:13)* The Acts of the Apostles and the Epistles give extensive testimony to the action of the Holy Spirit. Thus the faith of the Apostolic Church and the testimony of Scripture affirm the truth of the Holy Trinity.

1. What is the doctrine of the Holy Trinity?

"The Trinity is One. We do not confess three Gods, but one God in three persons, the 'consubstantial Trinity.'[15]" Thus the Church confesses, following the New Testament, 'one God and Father from whom all things are, and one Lord Jesus Christ, through whom all things are, and one Holy Spirit in whom all things are.'[16]" *Catechism, 253, 258*

2. Are the Son and Holy Spirit God?

"Following this apostolic tradition, the Church confessed at the first ecumenical council, at Nicaea (325) that the Son is 'consubstantial' with the Father, one only God with him."[17]

"The apostolic faith concerning the Spirit was confessed by the second ecumenical council at Constantinople (381): 'We believe in the Holy Spirit, the Lord and giver of life, who proceeds from the Father.'[18] ...'With the Father and the Son, he is worshipped and glorified.'[19]" *Catechism, 242,245*

3. Is salvation the mission of Father, Son and Spirit?

"The whole divine economy is the common work of the three divine persons. For as the Trinity has only one and the same nature, so too does it have only one and the same operation." *Catechism, 258*

As Catholics We Believe...

C. Some object that the word Trinity does not appear in the Bible. That is true, but the *reality* of Trinity is there and was believed by the Apostolic Church. The teachings of Arius and Nestorious and others were rejected by early Church councils. These councils did not create the doctrine of the Trinity, but reasserted the living faith of the Church. They developed language about person and nature to illumine the mystery. The Trinity has three divine persons and one divine nature. Unity in nature. Multiplicity in persons. One God, three persons.

Teachers today who speak of Christ as only human and not the Son of God act contrary to the living faith of the Church, held since the days of the Apostles. Faith in Christ's divinity is a key to faith in the Trinity.

We quoted Augustine's stirring words about how God called him. It was this same Augustine who gave the Church one of the deepest reflections ever on the most holy Trinity.

Reflection

It was with providence that I created you. When I contemplated my creature in myself I fell in love with the beauty of my creation. I provided you with the gift of memory so that you might be made a sharer in the eternal Father's power. I gave you understanding so that in the wisdom of my only-begotten Son, you might comprehend what I the eternal Father want. I gave you a will to love making you a sharer in the Holy Spirit's mercy.

—St. Catherine of Siena
Praying With Catherine of Siena,
by Patricia Mary Vinje, St. Mary's Press,
Winona, MN, 1990 pages 37-38

In My Life

1. As I meditate on Augustine's call from God, what details impress me most? How might I be drawn to my inner life to listen to God's call to me? Like Augustine, am I "deaf" to God's voice?

2. What imagery might I use to illustrate the mystery of the Trinity? How did St. Patrick use the shamrock for this purpose? How might I use the metaphor of water–ice–steam? Why should I realize that Trinity still remains mystery after my explanations?

3. Cite some passages from the New Testament which illumine the mystery of Trinity. How is the Trinity revealed in the Baptism and Transfiguration of Jesus?

"Make disciples of all nations, baptizing them in the name of the Father, and of the Son, and of the holy Spirit."

Matthew 28:19

Prayer

"O my God, Trinity whom I adore, help me forget myself entirely to establish myself in you. May nothing be able to trouble my peace or make me leave you. May each minute bring me more deeply into your mystery. Pacify my soul. Make it your heaven, your beloved dwelling and the place of your rest..."

Blessed Elizabeth of the Trinity, Catechism, 260

Glossary

Person—Center of responsibility. The "who" of an act. Who did it? Mary or John did it.

Nature—The source of an action. The "what" that acted. What did it? A man, an animal, the wind.

Chapter 7

The Creation
Fire and Snow, Bless the Lord

"Lightnings and clouds, bless the Lord;
praise and exalt him above all forever."
Daniel 3:73

The Canticle of Brother Sun
St. Francis of Assisi

Be praised, my Lord, for Sister Moon and the Stars!
In the sky You formed them bright and lovely and fair.

Be praised, my Lord, for Brother Wind
And for the Air and cloudy and clear and all Weather,
By which You give sustenance to Your creatures!

Be praised, my Lord, for Sister Water,
Who is very useful and humble and lovely and chaste!

Be praised, my Lord, for Brother Fire,
By whom You give us light at night,
And he is beautiful and merry and mighty and strong!

Be praised, my Lord, for our Sister Mother Earth.
who sustains and governs us,
And produces fruit with colorful flowers and leaves!

Be praised, my Lord, for those who forgive for love of You
And endure infirmities and tribulations.

Blessed are those who shall endure them in peace,
For by You, Most High, they will be crowned!

(From *The Little Flowers of St. Francis*,
Hanover House, Garden City, NY, 1958, page 317)

Are we naturally secular or essentially religious?

A. *Some say...*

It's the most natural thing in the world to wonder about the origin of the universe. People have always done so. And they still do. Current New Age thinkers argue that the world itself is God. The development of the world is the becoming of God. More concretely, "we" are the origin of the world. This is pantheism, a word based on the Greek "pan" (all) and "theos" (god). Hence everything is God.

In ancient times Manicheans and Gnostics believed that the world resulted from two forces, Good and Evil, Light and Darkness. The "god" of evil causes physical disasters like floods and earthquakes and moral evil such as sins of the flesh. The "god" of goodness generates the beautiful things of earth and the virtues of the soul.

Eighteenth-century Deists, as we studied in chapter one, admit God created the world but now has nothing to do with it. Modern materialists (Marxist socialists and Capitalist secularists) claim there was no origin to the world. The material earth has always been here. The present universe simply resulted from billions of years of the interplay of material forces which have always existed. They have replaced the eternal spiritual God with the eternal material world.

All these opinions show how interested people have always been about the origin of the world. The respondents here say, "God is not the origin of the universe."

B. *The Catechism Teaches...*

...that God, Father, Son and Spirit created the world and its inhabitants out of nothing.   "In the beginning, God created the heavens and the earth."[20] *Catechism, 290*

Revelation provides the true answer to our persistent questions: Where did we come from? What is our ultimate destiny? Revelation links creation with covenant and salvation, thus embracing the big picture about origin and destiny. In the Bible the God of the creation narrative is also the God of the covenant and the God who saves us in Jesus Christ and who lives with us, through the Spirit, in the Church and Sacraments.

God created out of love. Aquinas says, "When the key of love opened his hand, creatures came forth." God created us to be full of love and happiness. That reflects God's glory. "The glory of God is man fully alive," says St. Iraneus.

God freely created out of nothing. His loving wisdom alone

made it happen. He used no previous material. The world is not the product of necessity, blind fate or chance.

God created a world in the state of *becoming*, on a journey toward ultimate perfection. Divine providence means that God is guiding the world to becoming what it is meant to be. It is God who has planted a sense of purpose in the world and in the heart of humanity.

1. If God created the world out of nothing, what else can his creative power accomplish now?

"Since God could create everything out of nothing, he can also, through the Holy Spirit, give spiritual life to sinners by creating a pure heart in them[21] and bodily life to the dead through the Resurrection.... And since God was able to make light shine in darkness by his Word, he can also give the light of faith to those who do not yet know him."[22]   *Catechism, 298*

2. Since God is so great above us, can he be near us?

"God is infinitely greater than all his works.... But because he is the free and sovereign Creator, the first cause of all that exists, God is present to his creatures' inmost being: 'In him we live and move and have our being.'[23] In the words of St. Augustine, God is 'higher than my highest and more inward than my innermost self.'"[24] *Catechism, 300*

3. Does God give us any work to do in the world?

"To human beings God even gives the power of freely sharing in his providence by entrusting them with the responsibility of 'subduing' the earth and having dominion over it.[25] God thus enables men to be intelligent and free causes in order to complete the work of creation, to perfect its harmony for their own good and that of their neighbors.... God is the first cause who operates in and through secondary causes: 'For God is at work in you, both to will and to work for his good pleasure.'"[26] *Catechism, 307-8*

As Catholics We Believe...

C. The Catechism's rich teaching on God as creator and ongoing providence is the most satisfying answer to our questions about origin and destiny. Inadequate answers, mentioned above, have only partial insights. The Deists concentrate on our human responsibility for the world, but ignore our weaknesses and deny the glorious power we can receive from God.

The materialists emphasize the importance of the physical world and its potential, but deny the reality of our spiritual needs and hungers and so plunge us into anxiety and despair. The pantheists sense our divine destiny and our kinship with God, but in denying the distinction between creator and creature, they nourish our vanity and pride and rob us of real spiritual growth. The gnostics and manicheans (in modern form) are pessimists, overwhelmed by the world's evil. They recognize evil but do not admit redemption is possible. They settle for fashionable despair. All these answers have two common threads. God is not the creator. Salvation from sin and all that oppresses us is either achieved somehow by ourselves—or not possible at all.

The Problem of Evil

The Catechism deals with the problem of evil both in this section, in the story of the Fall of Adam and Eve and in the whole history of salvation. It asks the modern (and ever ancient) question, "If God is good, how can evil exist?" There is no quick answer to this. The entire content of Christian faith (creation, sin, God's loving covenants, the saving work of Jesus Christ, the gift of the Spirit, the Church, the sacraments and the call to heaven) is the response to the mystery of evil.

But why didn't God make a more perfect world? St. Thomas said he could have. We don't know. God's wisdom directed him to make a world in the state of becoming. This means some things appear and others disappear. Good exists with evil. Nature demonstrates constructive and destructive forces. Physical evil stands with physical good in a universe of becoming.

God decided to give angels and humans intelligence and free will. This creates the condition where corruption can and does happen. Both angels and humans have sinned. God can bring good from the consequences of evil. Evil is strong. Grace is stronger. "Where sin increased, grace overflowed all the more...." *(Romans 5:20)*

"We firmly believe that God is the master of the world and of its history. But the ways of his providence are often unknown to us. Only at the end, when our partial knowledge ceases, when we see God 'face to face,'[27] will we fully know the ways by which—even through the dramas of evil and sin—God has guided his creation to that definitive sabbath rest[28] for which he created heaven and earth." *Catechism, 314*

Reflection

So, my God, I prostrate myself before your presence in the universe which has now become a living flame. Beneath the lineaments of all that I shall encounter this day, all that happens to me, all that I achieve, it is you that I desire, you I await.

Pierre Teilhard De Chardin, *Hymn of the Universe*, page 29

In My Life

1. In reading Father De Chardin's spiritual reflection on a sunrise, how would I see the link with God's first act of creation, "Let there be light."? *(Genesis 1:3)* As I ponder the inadequate answers to the origin of the world, how does my faith in the truth of revelation help me respond to them with the vigor and enduring vitality of God's truth?

2. Because God started the universe out of nothing, how can God take me out of the "nothingness" of my sins and imperfections and make me a new creation? What areas of my life need this?

3. What must I do to acquire the great vision of revelation that encompasses creation, salvation and eternal destiny as the big picture in which I live my life? In facing the perennial problem of evil, what are the lessons from the whole of Scripture and Tradition I should keep in mind?

"How manifold are your works, O LORD! In wisdom you have made them all . . . ."

Psalm 104:24

Prayer

Mountains and hills, bless the Lord.
Stars of heaven, bless the Lord.
Angels of the Lord, bless the Lord.
Spirits and souls of the just, bless the Lord.
PRAISE AND EXALT HIM ABOVE ALL FOREVER.

(Read all of the Song of Daniel 3:52-90)

Glossary

Creation From Nothing—Revelation teaches that God created the world from nothing. No previous materials existed prior to creation.
Divine Providence—God created the world in a state of becoming, moving it to become what he meant it to be. Providence guides creation to this perfection. Secondly, God empowers us with responsibility for the world, working with him for the good of others and ourselves.

Chapter 8

Made in the Image of God

"You have made him little less than the angels..."
Psalm 8:6

He had always loved God.

Now Michelangelo could strive to visualize a God of such transcendence that everyone would cry out, "Yes! That is the Lord God!" He had always loved God. In his darkest hours he cried out, "God did not create us to abandon us." His faith in God sustained him. And now he must make manifest to the world who God was.

He had only to set down in drawings the image he had carried with him since childhood. God as the most beautiful, powerful, intelligent and loving force in the universe. Since God had created man in his own image, he would have the face and body of a man.

The first human whom God created, Adam, had surely been fashioned in his likeness. By setting forth *Adam, the son*, true creature of his father: magnificent in body, noble in thought, tender in spirit, beautiful of face and limb, archetype of all that is finest in heaven and on earth, *there* would be reflected *God the Father*.

God, in clinging white robe which matched his virile white beard, had only to hold out his right arm to Adam, to reach one, infinitesimal life-breath more, and man and the world would begin.

Irving Stone *The Agony and the Ecstasy*, Signet, New York, 1961,
Pages 537-8.

Can we have a good self image without reference to God?

A. *Some say...*

In every part of our culture, there is an appeal to love one's self in order to have a wholesome self image. It is assumed that this can be done without reference to God. In searching for cures for the obsessions and addictions which plague so many people, authorities argue that the first step must be the rebuilding of a positive self image. Virtually all these experts believe this can be done without God entering the picture.

The shelves of bookstores groan under the weight of hundreds of self-help books, all providing models, paradigms, charts, step-by-step processes for improving self worth. Rarely, if ever, do these works claim prayer, spirituality or divine help might be useful in creating a positive self image. Optimistically, they teach that we have within ourselves alone the capacity to save ourselves from the debilitating forces of negative self doubt, loss of self confidence and poor self worth.

The pervasive message, from all quarters, is that a poor self-image is the cause of drug and alcohol dependency (and other addictions) —and, the cure is a self generated journey to a positive self image.

It would seem, then, if this be true, that we do not need to think of God, or seek divine help when working on the improvement of our self worth.

B. *The Catechism Teaches...*

...God created us in His image and that our personal fulfillment is based on living as God's images with divine grace.

"'God created man in his own image, in the image of God he created him, male and female he created them.'[29] Man occupies a unique place in creation: (I) he is 'in the image of God'; (II) in his own nature he unites the spiritual and material worlds; (III) he is created 'male and female'; (IV) God established him in his friendship." *Catechism, 355*

To be an image of God means we must become that image more perfectly by acting as God's image. What are the five qualities we have as God's images? (1) A mind to know the truth. (2) A will to love goodness. (3) Freedom to act in reference to truth and goodness. (4) The gift of human dignity. (5) Being a person-in-communion, never totally isolated, always called to loving responsibility for others and to God.

We make practical our being images of God first by using our mind to seek the truth with confidence it can be known and then sharing and witnessing it to others. Second, by using our will power for love alone. This is best achieved by doing the will of God at all times. Third, by directing our freedom to do what we should, not just what we feel like doing. Fourth, by basing our self worth on the immaculate and beautiful image of God implanted on our selves. Fifth, by communion with God and others through constant acts of love and care. Thus, it is not enough to be an image of God. We should become who we are. The image must "take flesh."

1. How are we images of God?

"Of all visible creatures only man is 'able to know and love his creator.'"[30]

"Being in the image of God, the human individual possesses the dignity of a person...."

"The human person, created in the image of God, is a being at once corporeal and spiritual.... But 'soul'... refers to the innermost aspect of man, that which is of greatest value in him,[31] that by which he is most especially in God's image: 'soul' signifies the *spiritual principle* in man."

"The human body shares in the dignity of 'the image of God....'"

"It is the whole human person that is intended to become, in the body of Christ, a temple of the Spirit."[32]

"Man and woman were made 'for each other' ... he created them to be a communion of persons...." *Catechism, 356, 357, 362, 363, 364, 372*

2. Did God make the sexes equal?

"Man and woman have been *created*, which is to say, *willed* by God ... in perfect equality as human persons ... man and woman possess an inalienable dignity which comes to them immediately from God their Creator.[33]

"In marriage God unites them in such a way that, by forming 'one flesh,'[34] they can transmit human life.... By transmitting human life to their descendants, man and woman as spouses and parents cooperate in a unique way in the Creator's work."[35] *Catechism, 369, 372*

3. What does the Church say about Adam and Eve?

"The Church, interpreting the symbolism of biblical language in an authentic way, in the light of the New Testament and Tradition, teaches that our first parents, Adam and Eve, were constituted in an original 'state of holiness and justice.'[36] This grace of original holiness was 'to share in ... divine life.'[37]" *Catechism 375*

As Catholics We Believe...

All the modern emphasis on a proper self image is a true insight as far as it goes. Our faith tells us it simply does not go far enough. One of the most powerful foundational teachings of the Catechism is our creation as images of God. It is a theme that arises again and again, most strongly in Section One of the Catechism on the moral life—Life in the Spirit.

Hence it is a happy coincidence, culturally, that awareness about the importance of self image occupies so much attention today. With our faith we can build upon these insights—and even many of the processes—for awakening the truest understanding of self worth in the light of being images of God. The five qualities of being an image of God listed above can be wedded to popular consciousness so that people can be brought to genuine self worth and true fulfillment in God.

Many self-help books have useful hints for our self improvement. But we need much more. We need God-Help books, such as Scripture and the Catechism to bring us to the kind of fulfillment which is lastingly satisfying.

God creates Adam as Eve watches from the shelter of his arm. From the Sistine Chapel ceiling, painted 1508-1522 by Michelangelo.

Reflection

"In no way is God in man's image. He is neither man nor woman. God is pure spirit in which there is no place for the difference between the sexes. But the respective 'perfections' of man and woman reflect something of the infinite perfection of God: those of a mother and those of a father and husband."[38] Catechism, 370

In My Life

1. If I were Michelangelo how might I want to do God's creation of Adam in a modern format? What have I heard about acquiring a positive self image throughout my years of education? What have I done about it? What worked and what didn't?

2. Paragraph B lists five qualities of being God's image. How could I make each of these qualities practical points of behavior in my life? Which ones seem to be the most difficult and why?

3. Why are the teachings of most self-help books not enough for my ultimate fulfillment? What are some positive points they make which fit well with the Catechism's teaching about being God's image?

"Father . . . You made us in your own image, and set us over the whole world to serve you."

Roman Missal, EP IV

Prayer

Divine Creator, you have made the earth, sea and sky and its inhabitants. Over all these you have made us as the crown of your creation. At the same time you give us an awesome responsibility to live as your image: knowing, loving, free, full of dignity and persons in communion—to reach true fulfillment in you. Give us your Spirit that we may do this wisely and well.

Glossary

Images of God—We image God by knowing truth, willing good, acting freely in reference to truth and goodness, respecting our human dignity as God's gift and loving God and others as persons in communion.

Self Realization—Contemporary culture often speaks of this need to fulfill ourselves, to have real self worth. The Catechism teaches this can only be achieved by acting as images of God, with the help of the Holy Spirit.

Chapter 9

Original Sin —
Paradise Lost

*"You are free to eat from any of the
trees of the garden except the tree of
the knowledge of good and bad."*
Genesis, 2:16

O Little Birds, I Love You.
A Memory of Original Holiness

One day as St. Francis was walking among the trees the birds saw him and flew down to greet him. They sang their sweetest songs to show him how much they loved him. When they saw he was about to speak, they nestled softly in the grass and listened.

"O little birds," he said, "I love you for you are my brothers and sisters of the air. You ought always to love God and praise him.

"For think what he has given you. He has given you wings to fly through the air. He has given you clothing both warm and beautiful. He has given you the air in which to move.

"And think of this: You sow not, neither do you reap, for God feeds you. He gives you the rivers and brooks from which to drink. He gives you the mountains and valleys where you may rest. He gives you the trees in which to build your nests.

"You toil not, neither do you spin, yet God takes care of you. It must be, then, that he loves you. So, do not be ungrateful, but sing his praises and thank him."

Then the saint stopped. The birds sprang up joyfully. They spread their wings and opened their mouths to show they understood his words.

And when he blessed them, all began to sing. And the whole forest was filled with sweetness and joy because of their wonderful melodies.

William Bennett, (Condensed from his *The Book of Virtues*,
Simon and Schuster, NY, 1993 Pages 761-2

Are we born now deprived of Original Holiness?

A. **Some say...**
God established our first parents in a state of original holiness and justice. In symbolic language, the *Book of Genesis* 1-3 describes this grace and truth. As the history of the human race unfolded, with its wars, violence, hatreds, jealousies and other sins, some argued that humans are basically bad. Luther and Calvin taught we are intrinsically evil. They said Jesus came and covered us with his immaculate garment to make us pleasing for the Father to see.

Others, however, proposed that we are intrinsically good. The 18th century thinker, Rousseau, believed we are basically good. He spoke of us as "noble savages" like children of the forest, simple, innocent—just needing education and culture to bring out our goodness. In this optimistic view of human nature, all we need is educational enlightenment. This "theory of progress" means we will all get better and better in every way day by day.

It would seem that Calvin and Luther are too pessimistic. Rousseau is right. We are not born deprived of original holiness. We are born totally good. Education and positive thinking will develop the potential with which we were born.

B. **The Catechism Teaches...**
...that we are born deprived of original holiness and justice, because of the disobedience of our first parents. Augustine called this Original Sin. We have no right to original grace, but God's love made that possible for us through Christ's salvation.

We are not intrinsically bad as Calvin taught. Nor are we intrinsically good, as Rousseau claimed. We are "damaged goods," as Augustine taught. We are born deprived of original holiness because Adam and Eve disobeyed God. We have no "right" to the grace of paradise. It is always and only a divine gift of love. "God so loved the world that he gave his only Son, so that everyone who believes in him might not perish but might have eternal life." *(John 3:16)* Because of God's love and Christ's salvation, the Spirit of God can, through baptism, make us beautiful new beings, completely recreated in love and grace.

The best way to understand the Genesis account of the Fall of Adam and Eve and the promise and fulfillment of salvation, is to meditate on Paul's letter to the Romans, chapter 5. "Just as through one transgression condemnation came upon all, so through one righteous act acquittal and life came to all...Where sin increased, grace overflowed the more...." *(Romans 5:18, 20)*

We do not commit original sin. We inherit the deprivation of original holiness, caused by the original sin. We do, however, commit actual sins —pride, anger, lust, greed, sloth, gluttony, jealousy, etc.—and we need Christ's saving grace to be delivered both from original and actual sin. Baptism delivers us from original sin (and any actual sins we have committed prior to receiving the sacrament).

The sacrament of Reconciliation frees us from our actual sins after Baptism. The Sacrament of the Eucharist, our prayer life and our acts of love, justice and mercy nourish and deepen the graces of original holiness to which we have been restored. In the Church we live in "Paradise Regained."

John Calvin
(1509–1564)
Humankind as
intrinsically evil

1. What do we learn from Scripture about original sin?

"The account of the fall in *Genesis 3* uses figurative language, but affirms a primeval event, a deed that took place *at the beginning of the history of man.*"[39] *Catechism, 390*

A. "'Although set by God in a state of rectitude, man, enticed by the evil one, abused his freedom at the very start of history. He lifted himself up against God and sought to attain his goal apart from him' (GS 13:1)." *Catechism, 415*

B. "By his sin Adam, as the first man, lost the original holiness and justice he had received from God, not only for himself but for all human beings." *Catechism, 416*

C. "Adam and Eve transmitted to their descendants human nature wounded by their own first sin and hence deprived of original holiness and justice; this deprivation is called 'original sin.'

"We therefore hold, with the Council of Trent, that original sin is transmitted with human nature 'by propagation, not by imitation' and that it is ...'proper to each' (Paul VI, CPG 16)." *Catechism, 417,419*

2. What does our experience of death, suffering and evil lead us to conclude?

"Sin is present in human history; any attempt to ignore it or to give this dark reality other names would be futile." *(Catechism, 386)*

"We must... approach the question of the origin of evil by fixing the eyes of our faith on him who alone is its conqueror."[40] *(Catechism, 385)*

"Only in the knowledge of God's plan for man can we grasp that sin is an abuse of the freedom that God gives to created persons so that they are capable of loving him and loving one another." *Catechism, 387*

3. What are the effects of Original Sin and Christ's graces?

"As a result of original sin, human nature is weakened in its powers; subject to ignorance, suffering, and the domination of death; and inclined to sin...." *Catechism, 418*

"The victory that Christ won over sin has given us greater blessings than those which sin had taken from us: "where sin increased, grace abounded all the more (*Rom* 5:20)." *Catechism, 420*

C. *As Catholics We Believe...*

All evil is an absence of something that should be there. That is why we call original sin a "deprivation" of original holiness. Hence we reject Rousseau's vision of human nature as intrinsically good because he denies the "deprivation of holiness" and teaches a fundamental goodness of humanity that does not in fact exist. But we also disagree with Calvin and Luther whose view of human nature as essentially depraved—a vision that goes well beyond deprivation, claiming that no goodness or potential for goodness remains in us.

Humanity after the Fall is not a black hole covered over with Christ's light. God still loved us, though we were in a weakened state. We were still love-able, both able to love and be loved, but this could not save us from our sinfulness, selfishness and the deprivation of holiness. For this we needed Christ's graces which give us greater gifts than our first parents had. (See *Catechism, 420*)

Reflection

The six "wounds" of original sin

Baptism removes Original Sin. But its effects remain.
The two wounds of the body are: (1) its exposure to physical suffering: (2) its mortality, that is, death.
The four wounds of the soul are (1) Ignorance: The difficulty we have in knowing truth. (2) Malice: Inclination to think and do evil to others. (3) Weakness in the will: Disordered desire for pleasure. (4) Uncontrolled emotions: Feelings dominate our lives.

In My Life

1. When I think of evil what comes to my mind? When I think of sins, what comes to my mind? Is there any difference between my responses to these two questions? How would I deal with people who deny the reality of evil and sins?

2. What is the relationship between: **(a)** my experience of evil and sins with Original Sin; **(b)** the reality of Original Sin and the saving work of Jesus Christ; **(c)** Original Sin and its effects in my personal life; **(d)** Original Sin and Grace?

3. How does the opening story about St. Francis remind me of Original Holiness? Why are extreme views of human nature (Calvin's pessimism/Rousseau's optimism) inadequate ways of thinking about it? In examining my conscience how could I identify the "wounds" of Original Sin in my life?

"Where sin increased, grace overflowed all the more . . . ."

Romans 5:20

Prayer

Merciful Father, you have always loved us, even when we fell in the disobedience of our first parents. From the beginning, you promised us a Savior, who came to us in Jesus Christ, your Son. We are grateful beyond all measure for this ocean of grace and love in which you bathe us. You have made us a new creation so we can, with your help, achieve an even greater fulfillment that we had originally. We praise and glorify you!

Glossary

Original Sin—This describes both the sin of disobedience of our first parents, transmitted to us by propagation, and our being born deprived of the gifts and graces of original holiness and justice. The saving work of Jesus Christ restored us to holiness and justice. We experience this deliverance in faith and baptism.

Chapter 10

We Have Heard the Question: Jesus Is the Answer

"I believe in Jesus Christ, his only Son, our Lord."

Apostles' Creed

Never Tire of Hearing Jesus Spoken of. Never Weary of it.

It is still of the adorable person of Jesus Christ I am going to speak. Never tire of hearing him spoken of. Never weary of it. We have everything in Christ. Without him neither salvation nor holiness is possible

Even to think of Jesus, to look at him with faith brings us holiness. Christ is not only a model such as the artist looks at when he paints a picture. Neither can we compare the imitation of Christ to that superficial imitation attained by some when they copy the deeds and gestures of a great man or woman they admire.

Christ is more than a model. God is not content with a natural morality or religion. God wills us to act as children of a divine race. If Christ possesses all the treasures of wisdom, knowledge and holiness, it is that we may share in them.

You know the means of approaching him is faith. By faith we touch Christ. In this divine contact, little by little, our soul is transformed.

Each of our Lord's actions is not only a model for us, but also a source of grace. In practicing all the virtues, Jesus merited for us the grace to be able to practice these same virtues which we contemplate in him.

Abbot Columba Marmion
(adapted from *Christ the Life of the Soul.*)
Herder, St. Louis, 1925 Pages 60-1;73

Is not Jesus as model and moral teacher his greatest gift to us?

Some say...

A. Without a doubt Jesus is a model and example whom we should imitate. After the Bible, the most widely read book in the history of the Catholic Church is the *Imitation of Christ*, showing us how to follow the footsteps of the Master. It is said that to acquire virtues, we need the stories of virtuous people to inspire us. Now no one has ever been more virtuous than Jesus. So his greatest gift to us is the example of how to live a life of love, justice, mercy and compassion.

At the same time Jesus was an outstanding moral teacher. His Sermon on the Mount *(Matthew 5-7)* is the greatest sermon on moral behavior ever given. Even many non-believers admire Christ as a moral guide. The wisdom of Christ's moral teachings has inspired millions for centuries and continues to do so today. His ethical vision remains a guide for the perplexed and a sure light in a confusing world. Therefore, his greatest gift to us is not only his sterling example, but also his moral teachings.

The Catechism Teaches...

B. ...that Christ's greatest gift to us is grace: salvation *from* sin, and salvation *for* divine life as children of the Father, co-heirs with Christ and led by the Spirit.

No one will deny the essential and enormous value of Christ's example for our Christian lives. Nor in any way can we withdraw from the critical and essential place Christ's moral teachings have for our Christian behavior.

But Christ's example and teaching remain external without the core gift of Jesus which is grace—*divine life*. He won this for us by his saving work on the Cross and in the Resurrection. He

The paschal mystery of Christ's death and resurrection brings us grace and divine life.

makes it available for us in the Sending of the Spirit and Founding of the Church and Sacraments.

Grace and Divine Life empower us to be changed into the likeness of Jesus. He lives his virtues in us. He floods our minds with his moral teaching so we have the "mind of Christ." Thus Jesus lives in us the mysteries of his life on earth. The saints tell us that nothing else can give us greater happiness, joy, peace and personal fulfillment. Read the *Catechism 512-559* (The Mysteries of Christ's Life) to appreciate this compelling truth about Christ's greatest gift to us.

1. What shall we say of the "Mysteries" of Christ's life?

"Christ's whole earthly life—his words and deeds, his silences and sufferings, indeed his manner of being and speaking—is *Revelation* of the Father...."

"Christ's whole life is a mystery of *redemption*." *Catechism, 516-17*

2. How do we share in the mystery of Christ?

"Christ enables us to *live in him* all that he himself lived, and *he lives it in us....* We are called only to become one with him, for he enables us as the members of his Body to share in what he lived for us in his flesh as our model."

"In humbling himself, he has given us an example to imitate, through his prayer he draws us to pray, and by his poverty he calls us to accept freely the privation and persecutions that may come our way." [41] *Catechism, 521-520*

3. How is Jesus a "Sacrament"?

"His humanity appeared as 'sacrament,' that is, the sign and instrument, of his divinity and of the salvation he brings: what was visible in his earthly life leads to the invisible mystery of his divine sonship and redemptive mission." *Catechism, 515*

As Catholics We Believe...

In our previous lesson we dwelt on the Fall of our first parents, original sin and its effects. Along with original sin are the actual sins people committed after that. As a result, the great question and cry of humanity has been and is now, "Who will deliver us from this oppression of sin?" The answer is Jesus Christ, the Son of God, who became a man to save us by his life, death and resurrection.

Jesus saved us by his example, his teachings and his saving death and resurrection. The paschal mystery of his death and resurrection brings us the grace and divine life we need to be free *from* sin and free *for* assimilating his example and teachings into our life. The paschal mystery makes us a "new creation" and thus able to *interiorize* Christ's example and teachings in our souls and *exteriorize* them in lives of love, justice and mercy.

Reflection

We must continue to accomplish in ourselves the stages of Jesus' life and his mysteries.... For it is the plan of the Son of God to make us and the whole Church partake in his mysteries and to extend to and continue them in us and in his whole Church. This is his plan for fulfilling his mysteries in us.

—St. John Eudes,[42] *Catechism 521*

In My Life

1. Obtain a copy of the *Imitation of Christ*. Read a chapter each day, either upon getting up in the morning, or just before going to bed. Make this a lifetime habit. Why does this lesson say that Christ's grace is his greatest gift, thus making his example and moral teachings even more relevant for us?

2. Which scenes from Christ's life make the greatest impression on me? Which moral teachings of Jesus have the greatest impact on me? How can I tell from my behavior that Jesus is an influence on my life? How often do I advert to the power of Christ's graces on my life? What should I do to be more open to the graces of Jesus?

3. Which words of Abbot Marmion in the opening reflection motivate me the most? Why is it important to remember that only "faith" really gets in touch with Christ, that by "faith" my soul is little by little transformed by Christ?

"Oh, the depth of the riches and wisdom and knowledge of God!"

Romans 11:33

Prayer

Adorable Savior, Jesus Christ, you inspire us with your example and you enlighten us with your teachings. But without the graces, won for us by your paschal mystery, these essential gifts do not transform our inner souls. Give us then the mighty graces of salvation that you may live within us the mysteries of your example and your teachings. We praise you and love you.

Glossary

Mysteries of Christ's Life—Christ's example and teachings, as seen in the Gospels, are called mysteries, because they are not merely the acts of a human being, but the deeds of the Son of God become a man. Hence they are filled with divine mystery and power, which is made available to us by the graces that flow from his saving death and resurrection—the paschal mystery. Jesus is more than a model of holiness. Jesus causes holiness in us.

Grace—This rich term has several essential meanings. (1) It comes from the Latin word for gift. Grace is a gift of love and salvation from God. (2) Grace also means divine life which is communicated to us by The Holy Spirit. (3) Related to this, grace refers to the profound relationship we can have with Christ, in which his paschal mystery makes us a new creation, which in turn helps us to live Christ's example and teachings in our inner and outer lives.

Chapter 11

Blessed Be Jesus Christ, True God and True Man

"Is he not the carpenter's son?"
Matthew 13:55

"Thomas ... said to him, 'My Lord and my God!'"
John 20:28

Let Jesus Be Your Best Friend

"All blessings come to us through our Lord. He will teach us, for in beholding his life we find he is the best example. What more do we desire from such a good friend at our side? Unlike our friends in the world, he will never abandon us when we are troubled or distressed. Blessed is the one who truly loves him and always keeps him near.

Let us consider the glorious St. Paul: It seems that no other name fell from his lips than that of Jesus, because the name of Jesus was fixed and embedded in his heart. Once I had come to understand this truth, I carefully considered some of the lives of the saints, the great contemplatives, and found that they took no other path: Francis, Anthony of Padua, Bernard, Catherine of Siena...

Whenever we think of Christ we should recall the love that led him to bestow on us so many graces and favors, and also the great love God showed in giving us in Christ a pledge of his love; for love calls for love in return."

St. Teresa of Avila, *Liturgy of the Hours,*
Volume IV, pp. 1483-84

Isn't it better for our faith to focus on the humanity of Jesus?

A. **Some say...**

In a world where so many people are dehumanized by domestic violence, poverty, drugs, alcohol, sexual abuse and injustice, we need to have a human ideal to turn to. In a society so often lacking in compassion for the marginalized, we must have someone who will show us compassion. In a world where virtues have often disappeared, we need a paragon of virtue.

The humanity of Jesus responds to all these hungers. The gospels tell us he protected the humanity of the woman taken in adultery from the exploitation and hypocrisy of her accusers. Numerous gospel accounts show Jesus having compassion on the sick, the poor and the socially unacceptable people. The sacred texts give us a Jesus who modeled all the great virtues: love, prayer, courage, wisdom, justice, loyalty, honesty and hope.

Therefore, in our faith life, we should concentrate on the humanity of Jesus.

B. **The Catechism Teaches...**

...that we should focus on the Whole Jesus Christ, God and Man.

"The unique and altogether singular event of the Incarnation of the Son of God does not mean that Jesus Christ is part God and part man, nor does it imply that he is the result of a confused mixture of the divine and the human. He became truly man while remaining truly God. Jesus Christ is true God and true man. During the first centuries, the Church had to defend and clarify this truth of faith against the heresies that falsified it." *Catechism, 464*

In New Testament times and the first centuries immediately following them, the Church adhered to the biblical faith in Christ's humanity and divinity. But by the fourth century doubts arose. The Arians said Jesus was just a man who was later given a minor divinity status after the resurrection. The Monophysites claimed that Jesus was never truly human. God just assumed a human form, much as someone puts on a costume.

The Church's bishops fought these errors vigorously in four ecumenical Councils over a 125-year period. At Nicea in 325, they affirmed the traditional belief in the divinity of Jesus. At First Constantinople in 381, they upheld the divinity of the Holy Spirit. At

Ephesus in 431, they taught the reality of Christ's humanity and divinity and declared that Mary was truly the Mother of God, the *Theotokos* or God-bearer.

At Chalcedon in 451, the bishops repudiated the Monophysites claim that Jesus was never really human. The bishops affirmed the Church's traditional belief in Christ's humanity. The formula that emerged from these councils was that Jesus Christ was one divine person in two natures, human and divine. Jesus was not a human person, but he did have a human nature which meant he was really human. And he had a divine nature which meant he was really divine.

1. Did the Church always believe in Christ's divinity?

"From apostolic times the Christian faith has insisted on the true incarnation of God's Son 'come in the flesh.'" [43] *Catechism, 465*

2. How is the Son of God a man?

"'The Son of God... worked with human hands; he thought with a human mind. He acted with a human will, and with a human heart he loved. Born of the Virgin Mary, he has truly been made one of us, like to us in all things except sin.'" [44] *Catechism, 470*

3. How did Christ's humanity and divinity interrelate?

"Christ, being true God and true man, has a human intellect and will, perfectly attuned and subject to his divine intellect and divine will, which he has in common with the Father and the Holy Spirit." *Catechism, 482*

C. *As Catholics We Believe...*

The history of the Church is a story of cycles in which the faithful are drawn at one point to the divine aspect of Jesus and in another era to Christ's humanity. St. Francis of Assisi attracted people to the mystery of Christ's humanity as seen in the Christmas crib and the Stations of the Cross. But he never forgot Christ's dignity as Son of God. St. Thomas Aquinas drew people to contemplate the awesome majesty of Christ's divinity in his eloquent theological meditations. But that same Aquinas could melt hearts with his poetry about the Blessed Sacrament and the Gospel scenes of the Last Supper.

In an Eastern rite cathedral we are lifted out of ourselves to behold the divine Christ in heavenly glory, still bearing the nail marks of his humanity. In a Western rite country Church we gain the feeling of the Jesus of Galilee teaching and healing the rural crowds, without losing the sense of his divine Lordship.

The secret of our faith in the total Jesus Christ is to hold in our hearts both sides of his mystery. It is because he is divine that we have faith in him. It is because he is human that we identify with him, and through that humanity understand ourselves and get in touch with his saving power.

Pope Paul VI

Reflection

We wish, therefore, to tell you that the radical solution to your problems does not lie in a set of "things," but in "Someone." Someone in whom all the values you are secretly seeking are united: Christ. To all of you, we say: Go to meet Christ, the living Christ, whose voice rings out authentically in the Church today. Do not stop at the surface, but go beyond and gather the message, of which the Church is the reliable bearer, because she is assisted by the Spirit…If you wish really to be and remain always young, follow Christ! He alone is the Savior of the world. He alone is the true hope of all mankind.

Pope Paul VI, Address to Youth, February 25, 1978.

From *You Are the Future, You Are My Hope,* Speeches to Youth by Popes John Paul II and Pope Paul VI, Daughters of St. Paul, Boston, 1979, pp 306-307

In My Life

1. What seems most human about Jesus to me? Which of his virtues would I like to imitate and acquire? What plan would I devise to acquire these virtues?

2. Why is it important to me that Jesus be divine? Why does the Church remind me that my faith in Jesus flows from the truth about his divinity? Who are people that I know or have read about that have a strong faith in Christ's divinity?

3. Read again the opening selection in this chapter from the writings of St. Teresa of Avila. How does what she says about focusing on Jesus relate to my personal commitment to Christ? Why does she stress concentrating on Christ's love for us in any effort to be in touch with him?

"For to me life is Christ...."

Phil 1:21

Prayer

Dear Jesus, I join Thomas in adoring you as my Lord and my God. I also echo the great Councils of the Church that honored the truth of your humanity. I ask the Holy Spirit to keep these truths about you alive in my heart and to keep teaching me who you are and all that you mean to me and the world. I love you. Help my unlove. Praised be Jesus now and forever!

Glossary

Nicea—Church Council in 325 that affirmed divinity of Jesus.
Ephesus—Church Council in 431 that proclaimed Mary as *Theotokos*, God-bearer, Mother of God.
Chalcedon—Church Council in 451 that upheld the traditional Church belief in the humanity of Jesus.

Chapter 12

The Wondrous Cross—
The Easter Garden

"This man...you killed, using lawless men to crucify him. But God raised him up, releasing him from the throes of death...."
Acts 2:23-24

The Five Wounds of St. Francis

In the late summer of 1224 Francis of Assisi began forty days of fasting and prayer to prepare for the feast of the Exaltation of the Holy Cross. Just before this he asked Brother Leo to open the Gospels three times and read the first lines he found. Each time, Leo came upon a section from the story of the Passion and Death of Jesus. Francis chose those passages for his meditations on the heights of Mount Alverno.

One night an angel appeared to Francis in a dream. Carrying a violin, the angel said, "I will play for you as we play before God." The angel played only one note. It was so full of love and harmony that it moved Francis to say he thought his soul would go directly to heaven were he to hear another note. "My soul would have left my body with uncontrollable happiness."

At midnight when the feast of the Holy Cross began, he prayed for two favors. "I ask that I may feel the pain of Jesus in his Passion. I also ask that my heart be filled with the love that moved Jesus to the Cross in order to save sinners."

Then a fiery angel came from heaven. Wrapped in the midst of the fire was Christ crucified. The figure of the Crucified rushed upon Francis and touched him like a bolt of lightning. Francis felt his heart struck with God's love. He found on his hands, feet and side the imprint of Christ's five wounds. He felt the agony of Jesus even as he experienced the purest divine love.

Is faith a surrender to a person or a belief in a doctrine?

A. *Some say...*

"We bring you the good news that what God promised to our ancestors he has fulfilled for us, their children, by raising Jesus." *(Acts 13:32-33; NRSV)*. The resurrection of Jesus crowns our faith in him. The first Christian community believed in the resurrection and treated it as a central truth of faith. St. Paul preached this with enthusiasm, "If Christ has not been raised, then empty [too] is our preaching; empty, too, your faith." *(I Cor 15:14)*

Because Jesus has risen we can hope for the resurrection of our own bodies at the end of time. Because Jesus has risen we are now filled with divine life through Baptism and the Eucharist and the other sacraments. Because Jesus has risen, our faith is not in vain, but is a living faith in a living Lord. Our hunger for the total fulfillment of all that we are can now be satisfied. He rose from the grave to confirm our faith in his divinity and bring us eternal life. Our contemporary faith glows most brightly at the shrine of the Lord's resurrection.

The Risen Lord

B. The Catechism Teaches...

...that Christ's death and resurrection are essentially one saving act.

The Church speaks of Christ's saving action as the Paschal Mystery. It is a mystery because the Son of God performed it. It is also a mystery because some of God's glory is revealed to us, but most of God's glory remains hidden. It is called Paschal because it refers to the dying and rising of Jesus for our salvation. Resurrection could not happen if there were no death. His death would have been fruitless if there had been no resurrection. Good Friday must have an Easter Sunday. And we would have no Easter if there had not been a Good Friday. Christ's death overcame sin and death. Christ's resurrection brings us divine life and the promise of eternal life with God here and in heaven. There is an unbreakable bond between the death and resurrection of Jesus.

1. What did Christ's death accomplish?

"'Christ died for our sins in accordance with the scriptures' *(I Cor 15:3)*."

"The redemption won by Christ consists in this, that he came 'to give his life as a ransom for many' *(Mt 20:28)*, that is, he 'loved [his own] to the end' *(Jn 13:1)*, so that they might be 'ransomed from the futile ways inherited from [their] fathers' *(I Pet 1:18)*." *Catechism, 619,622*

2. What is the "justification" accomplished by Christ's resurrection?

"Justification consists in both victory over the death caused by sin and a new participation in grace.[45] It brings about filial adoption so that men become Christ's brethren, as Jesus himself called his disciples after his Resurrection: 'Go and tell my brethren.'[46] We are brethren not by nature, but by the gift of grace, because that adoptive filiation gains us a real share in the life of the only Son, which was fully revealed in his Resurrection." *Catechism, 654*

3. How does Christ's resurrection affect our own?

"Christ, 'the first-born from the dead' *(Col 1:18)* is the principle of our own resurrection, even now by the justification of our souls *(cf. Rom 6:4)*, and one day by the new life he will impart to our bodies *(cf. Rom 8:11)*." *Catechism 658*

"The Lord has truly been raised and has appeared to Simon!"

Luke 24:34

C. As Catholics We Believe...

When the risen Jesus appeared to the apostles and spoke to the doubting Thomas, he asked the apostle to touch the nail marks in his hands and the spear wound in his side. Even in his risen glory Jesus retained the evidence of his crucifixion and confirmed thereby the truth that his Cross was as essential as his rising to the work of redemption. Because it was the Son of God acting both at Calvary and at the garden tomb, the actions have eternal meaning. A divine person gave significance to the Cross and the resurrection.

The Jesus we meet in faith today is always "crucified and risen." We may never oversimplify what Christ has done for us. The complexity of his saving act ministers to the complexity of our need to die to sin and rise to new life. We can never prefer one half of the mystery to favor the other. It is the whole Jesus who saves us. We should respond with a faith that is whole and entire.

Reflection

"Christ's ascension marks the definitive entrance of Jesus' humanity into God's heavenly domain, whence he will come again (cf. Acts 1:11)....

"Jesus Christ, having entered the sanctuary of heaven once and for all, intercedes constantly for us as the mediator who assures us of the permanent outpouring of the Holy Spirit." Catechism, 665,667

In My Life

1. What personal stories can I share about sickness, death and tragedy? How were these experiences dealt with? What was my own reaction?
2. When I see a crucifix what thoughts come to my mind? What would I say to a Catholic who is made uncomfortable by the crucifix? Why is Christ's Cross important for my life?
3. What memories from my childhood do I associate with Easter? What does Easter mean to me today? How does my faith help me connect Good Friday and Easter?

Prayer

I adore you, O Christ, and I praise you, for by your holy Cross and resurrection you have saved the world. In my baptism I died to sin by my union with your death. And I rose to divine life by my union with your resurrection. Help me to live a life worthy of this great calling.

Glossary

Paschal Mystery—Refers to the saving death and resurrection of Jesus. We experience this mystery and its effects in the celebration of the sacraments.

Chapter 13

Breathe on Me, Breath of God

"Do not quench the Spirit."
I Thess 5:19

The Burning Mirror and Giant Windmills Image the Holy Spirit

In ancient times Archimedes built a giant solar reflector called the "burning mirror." It concentrated the sun's rays on Roman warships and set them afire. Primitive tribes used the sun to evaporate the ocean water they gathered in shallow pans, leaving salt behind. The coal and oil we use for energy comes from millions of years of converted sunlight. If 10,000 square miles of Arizona desert were covered with mirrors and the necessary boilers and turbines, it is estimated that America could double its electric power.

The wind also supplies us with energy. Wind powered the ships that brought Columbus to America and the pilgrims to Plymouth Rock. Old fashioned windmills used this free source of energy to grind wheat into flour. Today's scientists claim that armies of giant windmills in windswept areas like the Great Plains could produce one-fourth of our electrical needs.

The sun—that fire from the sky—provides us with phenomenal energy. The wind is a major energy source.

What are the images used to describe the manifestation of the Holy Spirit at Pentecost? Fire and Wind. God gives us fire and wind for our physical needs. God gives us the Holy Spirit for our spiritual needs. The Spirit is our spiritual solar furnace. He is the divine breath that sweeps our souls clean of sin and makes us feel brand new with grace. The Spirit gives us seven gifts: wisdom, knowledge, understanding, courage, counsel, piety, fear of the Lord. These are divine, renewable sources of energy for our souls.

Is it true that the Spirit's work did not begin until New Testament times?

A. **Some say**

The Old Testament reports the saving work of the Father. The Gospels communicate the saving work of the Son. The Acts and Epistles proclaim the saving work of the Spirit. After Pentecost the visible action of the Spirit is constantly preached and experienced.

On Holy Thursday Jesus told the apostles he was sending them the Holy Spirit to remind them of all he had said and done and to help them understand the message of salvation more deeply. On Easter Sunday night, Jesus appeared to the apostles in the Upper Room. His first act was to breathe on them and give them the Spirit. "Peace be with you.... Receive the holy Spirit." *(Jn 20:21-22)*

Powered by the Spirit, the apostles went forth to create a Church. They became the first Christian missionaries. When they faced their first crisis about requiring gentile converts to follow Jewish laws of circumcision and diet, they turned to the Spirit for guidance. "The whole assembly fell silent...." *(Acts 15:12)* They silently begged the Spirit for help. The Spirit guided them to dispense gentiles from such laws and opened the mission of the Church to the whole world.

In these and dozens of other instances the power of the Spirit was evident in the explosive life of the early Church. It was the Spirit who gave them courage to speak boldly about Christ and face martyrdom rather than deny their faith. Read St. Paul's first letter to the Corinthians, chapters 12-14, for an account of the abundant gifts with which the Spirit endowed the Church.

B. **The Catechism Teaches...**

...that the Spirit was at work from the beginning of Creation and continues to act in this "Time of the Church."

In the divine plan of salvation, the Trinity is at work at all times. Revelation unveils the work of each person. The Father appears in the act of creation and the preparation for the Messiah. The Son is manifested in the fullness of time. The Spirit is revealed in the "time of the Church," between the Ascension of Christ and his Second Coming.

Nonetheless, the Spirit was secretly working in our creation and for our salvation from the beginning. The Old Testament uses the expression "breath" to hint at the action of the Spirit. The Father "breathes" into a lump of clay and creates Adam. Jesus later would "breathe" on the apostles to give them life. The Father tells Ezekiel to invoke the four winds to bring life to the valley of dry bones. "From the four winds come, O spirit, and breathe into these slain that they may come to life." *(Ez 37:9)*

This text indirectly refers to the Holy Spirit.

1. What is the mission of the Spirit?

"The One whom the Father has sent into our hearts, the Spirit of his Son, is truly God[47]...When the Father sends his Word, he always sends his Breath....

"The mission of the Spirit of adoption is to unite them to Christ and make them live in him...." *Catechism, 689, 690*

2. In what areas of Church life do we see the Spirit?

" • In the Scriptures he inspired;
- In the Tradition, to which the Church Fathers are always timely witnesses;
- In the Church's Magisterium, which he assists;
- In the sacramental liturgy, through its words and symbols, in which the Holy Spirit puts us into communion with Christ;
- In prayer, wherein he intercedes for us;
- In the charisms and ministries by which the Church is built up;
- In the signs of apostolic and missionary life;
- In the witness of saints through whom he manifests his holiness and continues the work of salvation." *Catechism, 688*

3. How does the Spirit care for us?

"Through the Holy Spirit we are restored to paradise, led back to

the Kingdom of heaven, and adopted as children, given confidence to call God 'Father' and to share in Christ's grace, called children of light and given a share in eternal glory." [48] *Catechism, 736*

*The Descent
of the Holy Spirit
upon Mary and the Apostles*

C. As Catholics We Believe...

Our salvation from sin and our introduction into divine life and love is always a Trinitarian action, of Father, Son and Spirit. The visible manifestation of this saving action took place in stages, corresponding to our creation, history and readiness for such revelation in mind and heart. The three stages of salvation history are (1) preparation for the messiah; (2) the life, ministry, death and resurrection of Jesus Christ; (3) the "time of the Church" which is our own era that stretches from Christ's ascension to his second coming. It is in this third period that we see most clearly the action of the Holy Spirit.

We should be conscious of the Spirit's presence in our hearts, moving us to pray, to witness Jesus to our families, friends and the world, to be lights of divine love, compassion and forgiveness wherever the world is dark.

Reflection

"All of us who have received one and the same Spirit, that is, the Holy Spirit, are in a sense blended together with one another and with God. For if Christ, together with the Father's and his own Spirit, comes to dwell in each of us, though we are many, still the Spirit is one and undivided. He binds together the spirits of each and everyone of us,...and makes all appear as one in him. For just as the power of Christ's sacred flesh unites those in whom it dwells into one body, I think that in the same way the one and undivided Spirit of God, who dwells in all, leads all into spiritual unity."

St. Cyril of Alexandria,[49] *Catechism, 738*

In My Life

1. While I know the disadvantages of sun exposure on my skin, I am also aware of the sun's essential value to life on earth. What are some of those values? How could the sun's creative force image for me the Holy Spirit's positive contributions to my personal life?

2. The Bible uses the image of breath and wind to describe the life-giving work of the Spirit. What do I see in breath and wind which helps me appreciate how the Spirit works in me?

3. Read *I Corinthians 12-14*. Which gifts of the Spirit do I pray for? Which ones work in me? In Chapter 13, I read of the many ways the Spirit's gift of love appears. What must I do to internalize these many paths to love?

"The fruit of the Spirit is love, joy, peace, patience, kindness, generosity, faithfulness, gentleness, self-control."

Galatians, 5:22

Prayer

Come Holy Spirit and fill me with your seven gifts: wisdom, knowledge, understanding, courage, counsel, piety and fear of the Lord. Let each gift shape my conscience and drive away the seven deadly sins of pride, jealousy, anger, lust, sloth, gluttony and greed. Renew me at every moment of the rest of my life.

Glossary

Charism—A scriptural term used to describe God's gifts, especially the Spirit's gifts outlined in I Cor 12-14.

Paraclete—In John 16:7, Jesus calls the Spirit the Advocate or Paraclete, referring to the Spirit's work of convincing us of our sinfulness, convicting us of it, converting us from sin and consoling us in the process.

Chapter 14

The Church Is
the Body of Christ

"He [Christ] is the head of the body, the church."

Col 1:18

How Many Legions
Does the Pope Have?

Joseph Stalin

Hearing of Pope Pius XII's opposition to communism, Russia's autocratic dictator, Joseph Stalin, said, "How many legions does the pope have?" The pope had no army but he did have legions of saints and angels nourishing the spiritual forces that withstood and outlasted the "evil empire" that finally collapsed on Christmas Day 1990.

Church history is filled with accounts of kings, emperors and dictators confident of destroying the papacy and the church itself. In 1799 when Pope Pius V died, Napoleon was supposed to have said, "The papacy is finished." Things did look bad. The Papal States were occupied by the French army. The pope was imprisoned in the citadel at Valence where he died. The French Revolution and the Enlightenment appeared to have dealt a mortal blow to the Church.

The cardinals convened at a Benedictine abbey on an island near Venice. Protected by Austrian troops they took fourteen weeks to elect a new pope, Pius VII. For the next 23 years he led a spiritual renewal of the Church. A gentle and courageous man, he gladly offered refuge in Rome to the relatives of his fallen persecutor, Napoleon. At the abbey where he was elected we can now see a wall fresco of Pius VII giving his blessing to the world, along with the inscription, "Portae inferi non prevalebunt." (The gates of hell shall not prevail against the Church. *Cf. Mt 16:18*)

Is not the best image of the Church the "rock" or institution?

A. *Some say...*

At the base of the great dome of St. Peter's basilica are inscribed the words of Jesus to Peter, "Upon this rock I will build my church." (Mt 16:18) It would seem that the rock is the best image of the Church. Jesus had taught that we should build our houses on rock and not on sand.

In practical terms the organizational and institutional Church fulfills the meaning of being a rock. The Church as institution assures its *stability* in a chaotic and ever changing world. Secondly, the Church's institutional quality provides it with continuity through the centuries. How else could it have endured for 2,000 years? Lastly, the Church as rock gives its members a sense of confidence amid the confusions of life.

Without its institutional value the Church would not have been able to help its countless members who have brought their insights, ideas and charisms to the service of the Gospel to have an enduring impact. A great idea or charism needs to be channeled into a form which makes it available to a large number of people over an extended period of time. We call the process, "from charism to institution." Such is what happened to the genius of St. Benedict or St. Teresa of Avila. Benedict envisioned the value of monasticism. But he needed a Rule and an institution to give it shape and make it last to the 20th century. Teresa perceived the value of poverty and contemplative prayer. But without her Carmelite convents which institutionalized her gifts, her contributions would have died with her.

So it is with the Church as rock. Its organization encompassed the vision of Jesus Christ and the gift of the Spirit and gave that a way of journeying through 20 centuries to today.

B. *The Catechism Teaches...*

...that the Church is the people of God, the body of Christ and Temple of the Spirit. The Church is primarily a community that is served by its institutional traits.

"Christ is the light of humanity.... These words open the Second Vatican Council's *Dogmatic Constitution on the Church*. By choosing this starting point, the Council demonstrates that the article of faith about the Church depends entirely on the articles concerning Christ Jesus...."

"The article concerning the Church also depends entirely on the article about the Holy Spirit...." *Catechism, 748-749*

The word Church comes from a Greek word (ek-kalein) that means to convene an assembly of people, usually for a religious purpose. It is God who has called the Church into existence to **(1)** Hear his Word

(2) Listen with faith and obedience (3) Form covenant with him and (4) Experience salvation in Word and Sacrament and share this with the world. The English word Church comes from the Greek word Kyriake, meaning the "called community."

Vatican II says the Church is a "mystery." This means that it is created by God to be a Sacrament of Salvation. The Church is more than a sign of redemption. By the power of Jesus and the Spirit, it accomplishes the salvation for which it exists.

The Church is also the "People of God," a community called into existence by God. This community is the Body of Christ. Each member is a Temple of the Holy Spirit. Individually and communally the People of God, hear God's Word in faith and obedience, celebrate it in liturgy, live it in their moral and spiritual lives, serve the poor and the cause of love, justice and mercy and witness this by sharing their faith with all peoples.

Finally the Church is a hierarchy. The Father sent the Son to redeem the world. The Son sent the apostles to continue this mission. The Apostles sent the bishops to carry on the divine plan of salvation. The bishops, under the leadership of the pope and in communion with him, are the divinely appointed and Spirit guided teachers and shepherds of the Church. This is the rock, the institutional side of the Church.

1. What does the word Church mean?

"The word 'Church' means 'convocation.' It designates the assembly of those whom God's Word 'convokes,' i.e. gathers together to form the People of God, and who themselves, nourished with the Body of Christ, become the Body of Christ." *Catechism 777*

2. What is the external and internal meaning of the Church?

"The Church is both visible and spiritual, a hierarchical society and the Mystical Body of Christ. She is one, yet formed of two components, human and divine. That is her mystery, which only faith can accept." *Catechism 779*

3. How is the Church a Sacrament?

"The Church in this world is the sacrament of salvation, the sign and the instrument of the communion of God and men." *Catechism 780*

C. As Catholics We Believe...

Our Church is rich with meaning. This is why so many images and models are used to explore what the Church is all about. In catechesis, there are four marks or signs of the Church which have entered our tradition. These marks are yet another way to appreciate the gift of the Church which is one, holy, catholic and apostolic. What do these marks mean? Each mark is a reality that already exists, but is also a challenge to be achieved.

(1) The Church is One—The Church is one because she worships one Lord, confesses one faith, is born of one baptism, is given life by one Spirit for the sake of one hope of salvation. At the same time there is division between the Christian churches. Hence we have a moral commitment to the ecumenical movement to hear and obey Christ's prayer, "That they may all be one." *Jn 17:21*

(2) The Church is Holy—The holiness of the Church derives from the Father who created her, the Son who redeemed her and brought her holiness and the Spirit of holiness who communicates divine life to her. At the same time the membership of the Church includes sinners on the journey to holiness. Still, the Church has saints and boasts of the Blessed Mother in whom the Church is already all-holy.

(3) The Church is Catholic—This means the Church proclaims the fullness of the faith. The Church contains all the means of salvation. The Church is sent to evangelize all peoples in every age of history. The Church is "missionary" by nature.

(4) The Church is Apostolic—This refers to the fact that the Church is built upon "the twelve apostles of the Lamb." *(Rev 21:14)* The Catechism teaches that the Church "is indestructible (cf. *Mt* 16:18) She is upheld infallibly in the truth: Christ governs her through Peter and the other apostles, who are present in their successors, the Pope and the college of bishops." *Catechism 869*

Reflection

"There is not and there never was on earth a work of human policy so well deserving of examination as the Roman Catholic Church. The history of that Church joins together the two great ages of human civilization. No other institution is left standing which carries the mind back to the times when the smoke of sacrifice rose from the Pantheon, and when cameleopards and tigers bounded in the Flavian Amphitheater.

The proudest royal houses are but of yesterday, when compared with the line of Supreme Pontiffs. That line we trace back to an unbroken series from the Pope who crowned Napoleon in the nineteenth century to the Pope who crowned Pepin in the eighth; and far beyond the time of Pepin the august dynasty extended till it is lost in the twilight of fable...

She saw the commencement of all governments and of all the ecclesiastical establishments that now exist in the world; and we feel no assurance that she is not destined to see the end of them all. She was great and respected before the Saxon set foot on Britain, before the Frank had passed the

Rhine, when Grecian eloquence still flourished at Antioch, when idols were still worshiped in the temple of Mecca. And she may still exist in undiminished vigor when some traveler from New Zealand, shall, in the midst of a vast solitude, take his stand on a broken arch of London Bridge to sketch the ruins of St. Paul's."
Thomas B. Macaulay (Quoted in *The Faith of Millions*, by Father John A. O'Brien, OSV, Huntington, IN 1993 Pages 23-24)

In My Life

1. How long have I been a Catholic? How strong a Catholic am I today? How closely do I identify with the Catholic Church, its doctrinal and moral teachings and its call to regular participation in the Sunday liturgy? If I am a faithful and practicing Catholic, to what do I attribute this? If I am not, how can I improve myself in this regard?
2. If I were explaining the Church as both a community and an institution, what would I say? How are the marks of the Church relevant to my membership in the Church? If I want to share my faith with others, how would I go about it?
3. What do I know about the history of the Catholic Church? What should I do to learn more about it? Why is knowing its history a way of deepening one's faith?

"Since you are eager for manifestations of the Spirit, strive to excel in building up the Church."

I Cor 14:12 (RSV Translation)

Prayer

"Your heralds brought glad tidings to greatest and to least. They told all people to hasten to share the great King's feast; And this was all their teaching in every deed and word, to all alike proclaiming: One Church, One Faith, One Lord."

Hymn for Common of Apostles,
Liturgy of Hours, Volume 3, Page 1660

Glossary

Four Marks of Church—One, Holy, Catholic, Apostolic.
College of Bishops—The Communion of Bishops with each other under and with the Pope, the Bishop of Rome.

Chapter 15

Holy Mary, Mother of God, Pray for Us

From a Letter of St. Bernadette About Her Vision of Mary at Lourdes

St. Bernadette

"I had gone down one day with two other girls to the bank of the river Gave when suddenly I heard a kind of rustling sound. I turned my head toward the field by the side of the river but the trees seemed quite still and the noise was evidently not from them. Then I looked up and caught sight of the cave where I saw a lady wearing a lovely white dress with a bright belt. On top of each of her feet was a pale yellow rose, the same color as her rosary beads.

At this I rubbed my eyes, thinking I was seeing things, and I put my hands into the fold of my dress where my rosary was. I wanted to make the sign of the cross, but for the life of me I just couldn't manage it and my hand just fell down. Then the lady made the sign of the cross herself and at the second attempt I managed to do the same, though my hands were trembling. Then I began to say the rosary while the lady let the beads slip through her fingers, without moving her lips. When I stopped saying the Hail Mary, she immediately vanished.

I asked my companions if they had noticed anything, but they said no...I came back next Sunday, feeling myself drawn to the place...I went back each day for fifteen days and each time, except one Monday and one Friday, the lady appeared and told me to look for a stream and wash in it and to see that the priests built a chapel there. I must also pray, she said, for the conversion of sinners. I asked her many times what she meant by that, but she only smiled. Finally with outstretched arms and eyes looking up to heaven she told me she was the Immaculate Conception."

Text is from *Liturgy of the Hours, Feast of Our Lady of Lourdes*, February 11, Vol. III, pages 1375-76

(Bernadette died in 1879 at the age of 35. The Church canonized her a saint in 1933. The shrine at Lourdes is renowned for stirring up in millions of pilgrims a renewed faith in Christ and devotion to Mary and a zeal for prayer and charitable service to the sick and poor. It has also been the site of miracles of healing.)

Is Mary an intercessor for us or a model of faith?

A. *Some say...*

It seems clear that the Virgin Mary's value for us is her good example as a woman of faith. The New Testament portrays Mary as a woman who walked by faith from the Annunciation to Pentecost. She was totally responsive to the Father's will and always in accord with the saving purposes of her son. She followed the impulses of the Holy Spirit in every way.

In Scripture, faith means the surrender of the heart and body as well as the mind and will. St. Luke describes her as pondering "in her heart" the mystery of her son. *(Lk 2:19,51)* Just as she followed the divine will, she advised others to do the same. At Cana she said, "Do whatever he tells you." *(Jn 2:5)*

Mary consented in faith to be the mother of Jesus. Mary received the Word of God into both her heart and her body at the Annunciation. She conceived in her heart with her whole being before she conceived Jesus in her body. Mary's faith in God preceded her motherhood of God. By her faith Mary became the perfect example of what the Gospels mean by spiritual motherhood. When Jesus heard his mother praised for having borne him and nursed him, he replied, "Blessed are those who hear the word of God and observe it." *(Lk 11:28)* Mary is a model of faith and inspires us to be the same.

B. *The Catechism Teaches...*

...that Mary is the Mother of God, Mother of the Church, Model of Faith and an Intercessor on our behalf.

"What the Catholic faith believes about Mary is based on what it believes about Christ, and what it teaches about Mary illumines in turn its faith in Christ."

"The One whom she conceived as man by the Holy Spirit, who truly became her Son according to the flesh, was none other than the Father's eternal Son, the second person of the Holy Trinity. Hence the Church confesses that Mary is truly 'Mother of God' (*Theotokos*)." *Catechism, 487, 495*

Catholic devotion to Mary flows from Catholic faith in the meaning of Jesus Christ. Mary's whole mission in her life was to bring people to

Jesus. Her "yes" to the Father at the Annunciation made possible the conception of Jesus by the power of the Holy Spirit. Mary never draws attention to herself, only to Christ. "My soul proclaims the greatness of the Lord...." (*Lk* 1:46) The more hidden she becomes, the more visible her son.

Scripture portrays her in contemplative and prayerful terms. It is in the silence of her prayer that the angel Gabriel comes to her at the Annunciation. Our last glimpse of her in Scripture is at Pentecost, praying with the Church for the coming of the Spirit. Tradition says that she went to live with St. John in Ephesus. Her contemplative depths and prayer accompany John's first steps in the composition of his most prayerful of gospels. It could well be that Paul began his two-year evangelizing of Ephesus while Mary was still alive and probing more deeply the wells of prayer. If so, her intercession for him added divine power to his calling the Ephesians to faith in Christ. As Mother of God, a model of faith, prayer, contemplation and powerful intercession, Mary is the strong and valiant woman of the New Testament.

1. What is Mary's Immaculate Conception and Assumption?

"From among the descendants of Eve, God chose the Virgin Mary to be the mother of his Son. 'Full of grace,' Mary is 'the most excellent fruit of redemption' *(SC 103)*: from the first instant of her conception, she was totally preserved from the stain of original sin and she remained pure from all personal sin throughout her life."

"When the course of her earthly life was finished, [she] was taken up body and soul into heavenly glory.... The Assumption of the Blessed Virgin is a singular participation in her Son's Resurrection and an anticipation of the resurrection of other Christians...." *Catechism, 508, 966*

2. Was Mary always a virgin?

"The deepening of faith in the virginal motherhood led the Church to confess Mary's real and perpetual virginity even in the act of giving birth to the Son of God made man.[50] In fact, Christ's birth 'did not diminish his mother's virginal integrity but sanctified it.'[51] And so the liturgy of the Church celebrates Mary as *Aeiparthenos*, the 'Ever-virgin.'"[52] *Catechism, 499*

3. Does Mary pray for our needs? What is Marian devotion?

"...by her manifold intercession [Mary] continues to bring us the gifts of eternal salvation.... Therefore the Blessed Virgin is invoked in the Church under the titles of Advocate, Helper...."

"'The Church's devotion to the Blessed Virgin is intrinsic to Christian worship.'[53] ...'This very special devotion...differs essentially from the adoration which is given to the incarnate Word and equally to the Father and the Holy Spirit, and greatly fosters this adoration.'[54] The liturgical feasts dedicated to the Mother of God and Marian prayer, such as the rosary, an 'epitome of the whole Gospel,' express this devotion to the Virgin Mary."[55] *Catechism 969, 971*

C. As Catholics We Believe...

The history of the Catholic Church gives undeniable evidence that vibrant faith in Jesus is always accompanied by a living devotion to Mary. Departure from Mary means a cooling of relationship with Jesus. Mary does not want a concentration on her for her own sake, but only for the sake of her Son. And all of this is for our salvation, our happiness and holiness.

Of her many titles, the one that emerged from the days of Vatican II contains this perennial Catholic teaching in a fresh way. That is her title as "Mother of the Church." "She is 'clearly the mother of the members of Christ'... since she has by her charity joined in bringing about the birth of believers in the Church, who are members of its head.'[56] 'Mary, Mother of Christ, Mother of the Church.'"[57] *Catechism, 963*

Reflection

In the following words, Thomas Merton imagines Mary's journey to visit her cousin Elizabeth:

You have trusted no town
With the news behind your eyes,
You have drowned Gabriel's word in thoughts like seas
And turned toward the stone mountain
To the treeless places.
Virgin of God, why are your clothes like sails?
The day Our Lady full of Christ,
Entered the dooryard of her relative
Did not her steps, light steps, lay on
the paving leaves like gold?
Did not her eyes grey as doves
Alight like the peace of a new world upon that house,
upon miraculous Elizabeth?

Thomas Merton, The Quickening of St. John the Baptist,
from his book, The Tears of the Blind Lions.

In My Life

1. How vital is the presence of the Blessed Mother in my faith life? Do I ever recite the Rosary? Do I know how to say the Rosary? How do I connect my realtionship with Mary with my faith in Jesus?

2. In my resolve to offer my chastity as a gift to my spouse in marriage, how can the Blessed Virgin help me? If, unhappily, I have not kept my chastity, how can I be reborn in holy purity and remain in it with the assistance of the Virgin Mary?

3. After Jesus himself, the greatest example of a prayerful person is his Blessed Mother. What can Mary do for me to develop a rich prayer life? When I begin to experience Mary as my spiritual mother, what will that mean for my faith in Jesus? What practices of devotion to Mary will help me have a more intense relationship to Jesus?

"All these devoted themselves...to prayer, together with some women, and Mary the mother of Jesus...."

Acts 1:14

Prayer

All-holy Mary, ever a virgin and mother of God, I turn to you for help. Pray for me that I may draw closer to Jesus. Pray for me that I may prize the virtue of chastity. Pray for me that I may become a person of prayer. Show me the depth of your faith in Jesus that my unbelief may turn into ardent faith in Christ.

Glossary

Immaculate Conception—The Church's teaching that Mary was conceived without original sin by the anticipated merits of Jesus Christ and that she lived her full life without sin.

Mary's Glorious Assumption—At her death, Mary was taken up body and soul to heaven. Mary's resurrection is an anticipation of the resurrection of the body of other Christians.

Ever Virgin—The Church's faith that Mary was not only a virgin in conceiving and bearing Jesus but that she remained so for the rest of her life. This teaching was upheld by St. Ambrose at the Council of Capua in 392.

Chapter 16

Death and Judgment

"The wages of sin is death."
Romans 6:23

Just outside of Cairo is the world's biggest tombstone. It is a pyramid as high as a fifty story building. Over two million blocks of stone, each weighing two and one-half tons went into this building. 100,000 men quarried the stones, transported them to the site and elevated them into place. The base of the pyramid is square, each side the length of three football fields. This was the most expensive tomb ever built—and all of it to house the body of one pharaoh.

If nothing else, the pyramid demonstrates how seriously people take death and come to terms with its mystery. Death rituals try to deal with human concerns: (1) The living wish to be free from the contamination of death. (2) The dead should be allowed to find rest. (3) The survivors need ways to adjust to the loss of a loved one.

What should be done with the body? Hindu and Buddhist cultures call for cremation. Western cultures practice burials, though cremation is increasingly becoming popular. The Parsees of India had another method. They constructed *Towers of Silence,* wooden towers on top of which they placed the bodies where vultures and other birds of prey could devour the flesh. The bones were then gathered and buried.

Then there is the wake. Folklore and song have preserved what is known as the Irish wake. Scholars believe this custom was a holdover from the medieval custom of "rousing the ghost" in the hope of bringing the person back to life.

Today we have the beautiful revised Catholic liturgy of Christian burial. The paschal candle, symbolizing death and resurrection, stands near the coffin. The coffin is covered with a festive white and gold cloth to recall the person's baptism, the beginning of the faith journey and its fulfillment now in eternal life. The prayers and hymns are filled with resurrection themes. "Life is changed, not taken away," says the Preface. The immortality of the soul is celebrated and the future resurrection of the body prayed for. Nowhere else in our modern society is death treated with more dignity, hope, reverence and beauty. Tears and mourning are welcomed, but in an environment of Christian hope.

Egyptian pyramids were built as tombs for the pharaohs.

Is the soul judged immediately after death?

Some say...

Scripture seems to speak only of a general judgment at the end of time. In Matthew 25, Jesus tells of the Last Judgment when the Son of Man will come in glory. "All the nations will be assembled before him. And he will separate them one from another, as a shepherd separates the sheep from the goats." *(Mt 25:32)* Those who have fed the hungry, clothed the naked, visited the prisoners and gave a cup of water to the thirsty will go to heaven. Those who did not do this will go to hell. "These will go off to eternal punishment...." *(Mt 25:46)* Our future destiny depends on how we treated people here, for "Whatever you did for one of these least brothers of mine, you did for me." *(Mt 25:40)*

B. *The Catechism Teaches...*

...there is both a particular judgment right after death and a general judgment at the Second Coming of Jesus.

"The New Testament speaks of judgment primarily in its aspect of the final encounter with Christ in his second coming, but also repeatedly affirms that each will be rewarded immediately after death in accordance with his works and faith. The parable of the poor man Lazarus and the words of Christ on the cross to the good thief, as well as other New Testament texts speak of a final destiny of the soul—a destiny which can be different for some and for others." [58] *Catechism, 1021*

It is the soul that immediately survives death. The body will join the soul at the general resurrection of the dead.

Hence our particular judgment occurs right after death. The general judgment confirms this again when our souls are joined with our bodies. From one point of view, we bring judgment upon ourselves by the way we have lived. From another aspect God is judging us, but his judgment simply confirms what we have already done with our own lives. We were given freedom to act lovingly, justly and mercifully to all. We were also given all the graces needed to do so. This occurred in the gift of the Spirit and his multiple graces to help us to salvation. We experienced these gifts of grace in the Church, the community of faith, the celebration of the sacraments, the numerous acts of love directed to us by others and the prayers of Mary and the saints. We were responsible for our lives on earth. After death we must accept the consequences of our behavior. If we cooperated with grace, we will go to heaven. If we did not, then we face eternal damnation.

1. What is heaven?

"Those who die in God's grace and friendship and are perfectly purified live for ever with Christ. They are like God for ever, for they 'see him as he is,' face to face...." [59]

"This perfect life with the Most Holy Trinity—this communion of life and love with the Trinity, with the Virgin Mary, the angels and all the blessed—is called 'heaven.' Heaven is the ultimate end and fulfillment of the deepest human longings, the state of supreme, definitive happiness." *Catechism, 1023-24*

2. What is purgatory?

"All who die in God's grace and friendship, but still imperfectly purified, are indeed assured of their eternal salvation; but after death they undergo purification, so as to achieve the holiness necessary to enter the joy of heaven."

"The Church gives the name *Purgatory* to this final purification of the elect...."

"This teaching is also based on the practice of prayer for the dead, already mentioned in Sacred Scripture: 'Therefore [Judas Maccabeus] made atonement for the dead, that they might be delivered from their sin.'" [60] *Catechism, 1030-32*

3. What is hell?

"We cannot be united with God unless we freely choose to love him. But we cannot love God if we sin gravely against him, against our neighbor or against ourselves: 'He who does not love remains in death. Anyone who hates his brother is a murderer, and you know that no murderer has eternal life abiding in him.' [61] Our Lord warns us that we shall be separated from him if we fail to meet the serious needs of the poor and the little ones who are his brethren.[62] To die in mortal sin without repenting and accepting God's merciful love means remaining separated from him for ever by our own free choice. This state of definitive self-exclusion from communion with God and the blessed is called 'hell.'" *Catechism, 1033*

C. *As Catholics We Believe...*

The Church has traditionally spoken of the "Last Things"— Death, Judgment, Heaven and Hell. We are urged to prepare for a truly Christian death that goes beyond denial, anger, bargaining and depression. We should arrive at a faith acceptance of our death in union with Christ on the Cross who said, "Father, into your hands I commend my spirit." *(Lk 23:46)* How we lived on earth determines whether we go to heaven or hell and whether we spend some time in purgatory. Our daily lives distract us from these final realities, yet what we do today influences how our life story will turn out in the world to come.

Reflection

"Go forth, Christian soul from this world...
May you live in peace this day,
may your home be with God in Zion...
May you return to [your Creator]
who formed you from the dust of the earth.
May holy Mary, the angels, and all the saints
come to meet you as you go forth from this life...
May you see your Redeemer face to face..."
Prayer of Commendation at Christian Burial.

In My Life

1. What experiences of death have I had? With my family? My friends? What impact did that have on me? When I think about my own death what comes to my mind? If I imagined myself in my coffin, what would I like people to say about me when they came to pay their respects?

2. When I imagine heaven what do I think about? What must I do here in order that I might go to heaven? Why is thinking of my final destiny important for what I do today? How often do I pray for the souls in purgatory? How could I improve my spiritual concern for departed relatives and friends?

3. What must I do to avoid going to hell? Name the many spiritual resources I have as a member of the Church to help me avoid hell. How aware am I of my sinfulness? How faithful am I to the practice of confession?

"Remain faithful until death, and I will give you the crown of life." *Rev. 2:10*

Prayer

Lord of life, you came to give us life here and hereafter. You died on the Cross to conquer death and make us fully alive. It was your love that overcame death. It is your will that love should permeate my every moment so that I can live abundantly here on earth and have eternal life in heaven. Fill me with your Holy Spirit of life so that everything I touch thrills with life and everyone I meet comes alive because of love.

Glossary

General Judgment—The judgment on every human being that will occur at the second coming of Jesus.

Particular Judgment—The judgment each of us receives at the moment of death. Our souls experience this judgment. They will be united to our bodies at the final resurrection of the dead at Christ's second coming.

Heaven—A state of absolute happiness due to our union with the Holy Trinity in the company of the Blessed Mother the angels and all the blessed.

Hell—A state of eternal suffering due to our self-exclusion from God by means of our sins against God, others, self.

Purgatory—A temporary state of purification prior to going to heaven.

Chapter 17

The Celebration
of the Christian Mysteries

"Offer spiritual sacrifices
acceptable to God through Christ Jesus."
I Peter 2:5

When the Mystery of Faith
Coincided With
the History of Faith

In April 1991, hundreds of Catholics packed St. Yuri's cathedral in Lvov, Ukraine for the first Catholic Easter Mass there in 43 years. The Communist government had returned the church to the Catholics and they came to celebrate. On Holy Saturday evening, they assembled in the church at 11 pm. At 11:45 pm they left the church and went in procession around the outside of the building singing hymns whose words yearned for the resurrection of Jesus.

Having made the circle the procession returned to the closed door of the cathedral. The deacon sang the Easter gospel. When he came to the words of the angel to the women, "Why look you for the living among the dead? He is risen! He is not here," Cardinal Lubachivsky sang out "Christos Voskrese!" (Christ is risen!) All the people replied, "Voistinu Voskrese!" (He is risen indeed!)

The doors of the cathedral opened and the joyful throng flowed into the church filling every corner of the building. Then followed five hours of liturgy, reading, singing, processing, the consecration of the Eucharist and Communion. Here was a clear case of the mystery of faith coinciding perfectly with the history of faith. They celebrated the resurrection of Jesus at the very moment that their whole Ukrainian Church of six million people were rising from the death of persecution after 43 years.

Liturgy is always celebrating the mighty deeds of God in history, especially those revelation events recounted in the Bible. In a very real way this liturgy solemnized another mighty act of God saving his people from persecution and extinction. The alleluias that rang out in that cathedral had a very personal meaning for those worshipers.

Is liturgy a matter of fellowship or sacrifice?

A. *Some say...*
We have already seen that the Church is a called community in which the Father gathers the people to hear and obey his word, form covenant with him and celebrate and remember salvation in community worship. Liturgy is a supreme moment in the fellowship life of the Church. God's people gather in Christ's name to express their faith and fellowship ties with each other. The Body of Christ assembles for prayer. Christ is present in the proclaimed Word of Scripture, the altar on which the rituals of Eucharist are enacted and in the "assembly" around the altar.

The Fathers of the Church often said, "The Body of Christ in the Eucharist builds up the Body of Christ which is the Church." Liturgy is a powerful way of establishing a community based on the love of Christ. We say that the family which prays together stays together. Families which make liturgy an essential part of their lives draw on the cohesive power of worship for family unity as well as unity with others in the parish community

B. *The Catechism Teaches...*
...that liturgy is an action in which the Father blesses us, the Son enacts his *Paschal Sacrifice* and the Spirit teaches us the Word, communicates salvation to us and forms us into a faith community. *Liturgy includes sacrifice and community.*

The liturgy of the Eucharist is an action of the whole Christ, Jesus and all the members of the Church, each contributing according to the role assigned. By ordination the priest, in the person of Christ and through the power of the Spirit, makes the paschal mystery present in the transformation of the bread and wine into the body and blood of Christ. The assembly joins the priest in offering this sacrifice of praise to the Father.

The words, deeds, hymns, rituals, processions, gestures all form the liturgical action, each part giving meaning to the other. Liturgy is a kind of poetry in motion, a unified act in which the participants hear the Word of God, listen to its application, engage in the liturgy of the Sacrament and commune in the body and blood of Christ.

The Holy Trinity is both the origin and destiny of liturgy. Each person of the Trinity acts at liturgy and draws us into the heavenly life of God. Our liturgy on earth is a visible participation of the liturgy of heaven where Mary, the angels and saints engage in a communion of love for and praise of the Trinity. When we depart from liturgy we are commissioned to love and serve God by bringing love, justice and mercy to our families, friends and the world at large.

1. What is the Trinity's work at liturgy?

"In the liturgy of the Church, God the Father is blessed and adored as the source of all the blessings of creation and salvation...."

"Christ's...mystery of salvation is made present there by the power of his Holy Spirit...."

"The mission of the Holy Spirit in the liturgy of the Church is to prepare the assembly to encounter Christ ... to make the saving work of Christ present and active by his transforming power...." *Catechism 1110-1112*

2. What are the sacraments?

The sacraments are efficacious signs of grace, instituted by Christ and entrusted to the Church, by which divine life is dispensed to us. The visible rites by which the sacraments are celebrated signify and make present the graces proper to each sacrament. They bear fruit in those who receive them with the required dispositions.

3. Who celebrates liturgy? How, when and where?

"The liturgy is the work of the whole Christ, head and body...."

"In a liturgical celebration, the whole assembly is *leitourgos*, each member according to his own function...."

"The liturgical celebration involves signs and symbols relating to creation ... and the history of salvation...."

"The Liturgy of the Word is an integral part of the celebration...."

"Song and music are closely connected with liturgical action...."

"Sunday... is the pre-eminent day of the liturgical assembly, the day of the Christian family, and the day of joy and rest from work...."

"In its earthly state the Church needs places where the community can gather...."

"It is in these churches that the Church celebrates public worship...." *Catechism, 1187-1193, 1198-1199*

C. As Catholics We Believe...

We should never forget the centrality of God at liturgy. Without God there simply would be no liturgy. The whole point at liturgy is to recall God's blessings and saving acts, both in past history and now made sacramentally present for us. When God is forgotten at liturgy then the sense of reverence is lost and the feeling for the sacred dries up.

We live in a time when there is excessive attention to the things of earth and to our own narcissistic needs. Yet we only grow by getting beyond ourselves. We are only saved by a power that is transcendent. We must recover the joy of adoration and praise of the infinite God. Then our own souls stretch to contain unimagined beauty, grace and wonder and salvation.

Reflection

There is a market-square quality to Russian and Ukrainian churches, as though the people were happily shopping for saints, putting donations in boxes, buying and lighting candles, bowing blessing, praying, kissing icons, kneeling, singing in harmony and gazing with concentrated attention on their favorite icons. Their icons are more than pictures of Christ, Mary and the saints. They are windows that open the beholder to the sacred, to the very world of heaven itself.

Russian icon dating from the 16th century

In My Life

1. When I attend liturgy do I go there to give something of myself or mainly to get something out of it? If Jesus offers us his body to be given for others and his blood to be poured out for salvation, what practical outcome should that have for me?

2. While I enjoy the fellowship at Mass and the pleasant community feeling and hospitality, how can I focus on the other aspect, which is attention to God? How does the loss of the sense of the sacred in our culture affect even our worship experience?

3. When I hear that a sacrament is an effective sign, how would I explain that to someone else? How is my faith deepened at liturgy? Why does the priest send us on mission (Go and serve the Lord) at the end of Mass?

"Offer to God praise as your sacrifice...."

Ps 50:14

Prayer

At liturgy, O Father, I thank you for your blessings of creation and salvation. I thank you, Jesus Christ, for the paschal mystery of death to sin and life in God. I thank you, Holy Spirit, for making these blessings of salvation present for me.

Glossary

Liturgy—Originally from the Greek, meaning people's work. For us it means that celebrations of sacraments are the actions of the priest and the assembly—a symphony of words, deeds, symbols, music, art, gestures and movement, all directed to praising God.

Chapter 18

Born Again
in Water and the Spirit

*"No one can enter the kingdom of God
without being born of water and Spirit."*
John 3:5

Edith Stein Was Born Again
in the Catholic Church

Edith Stein was the eleventh child of a Jewish family, born in 1891 in Breslau, Germany. Her family was devout and religiously observant. By the age of 15 Edith had given up her religion and all practice of faith and prayer. She had a talent for philosophy and went to study under the greatest philosopher of the day, Edmund Husserl. He pronounced her his best student and brought her with him as his assistant when he went to teach at the University of Freiberg.

Though Edith had become an agnostic regarding religion, she was energetically honest in her search for truth. "Whoever seeks the truth," she wrote, "seeks God whether she knows it or not." Her search brought her to the autobiography of the great mystic, St. Teresa of Avila. When she closed the book after reading it all through the night, she said, "That is the truth."

She decided to become a Catholic and was baptized on New Year's Day 1922 at age 31. She resigned her post with Husserl and went to teach at the Dominican sisters' school in Speyer. Gradually she experienced a call to the Carmelite Order and was received into the Carmel at Cologne. In 1939, she transferred to the Carmel at Echt in Holland.

In 1942 the Dutch bishops denounced the Nazi persecution of Jews. In reprisal, the Nazis sent 1,200 Jewish Catholics to the death camps. Included among them was Edith Stein, now Sister Benedicta of the Cross. She was taken to Auschwitz. In August she was hurled naked into the gas chamber, after which her body was burned in the ovens. Pope John Paul II beatified her at a ceremony in Cologne in 1987.

Does baptism cleanse us from sin or initiate us into the Church?

A. *Some say...*

Baptism, Confirmation and the Eucharist belong to what the Church calls the "Sacraments of Initiation." These sacraments receive this title because they are given to those who are brought into the Church at the Easter Vigil. Converts to the Church are taken through a lengthy process—usually nine months—in a process called "The Rite of Christian Initiation of Adults (RCIA)."

Baptism is the first of these sacraments and it introduces us into membership in God's family, the Church. At the RCIA, Confirmation immediately follows this rite. If, on the other hand, the convert was already legitimately baptized in another Christian church, then only Confirmation is given at the vigil. The tradition of baptizing babies dates from the earliest days of Christianity when whole families, adults and infants alike, were brought into the Church.

B. *The Catechism Teaches...*

...that Baptism, Confirmation and Eucharist are sacraments of initiation. Baptism cleanses us from all sin, original and actual, and initiates us into divine life and membership in the Church.

"The sacraments of initiation—Baptism, Confirmation, and the Eucharist—lay the *foundations* of every Christian life. The sharing in the divine nature given to men through the grace of Christ bears a certain likeness to the origin, development, and nourishing of natural life. The faithful are born anew by Baptism, strengthened by the sacrament of Confirmation, and receive in the Eucharist the food of eternal life.' [63]" *Catechism, 1212*

While it is perfectly clear that Baptism initiates us into the life of the Church, it should also be recalled that this sacrament liberates us from original and actual sin. Baptism is a death to sin–resurrection to grace experience. "We were indeed buried with him [Jesus] through baptism into death [to sin], so that, just as Christ was raised from the dead by the glory of the Father, we too might live in newness of life." *(Rom 6:4)*

In Confirmation, the baptized are more perfectly bound to the Church and enriched with the special strength of the Holy Spirit. The result is that the confirmed are more strictly obliged to spread and defend the faith by word and deed. (Because of the centrality of the Eucharist, this sacrament of initiation will be treated at full length in the next chapter.)

1. What is Baptism?

"Baptism is birth into the new life in Christ...."

"The fruit of...baptismal grace is a rich reality that includes forgiveness of original sin and all personal sins, birth into life by which man becomes...a member of Christ and a temple of the Holy Spirit. By this very fact the person baptized is incorporated into the Church... and made a sharer in the priesthood of Christ." *Catechism, 1277, 1279*

2. What is Confirmation?

"Confirmation perfects Baptismal grace; it is the sacrament which gives the Holy Spirit in order to root us more deeply in the divine filiation, incorporate us more firmly into Christ, strengthen our bond with the Church, associate us more closely with her mission, and help us bear witness to the Christian faith in words accompanied by deeds." *Catechism, 1316*

3. How many sacraments are there and how do they correspond to our life cycle?

"Christ instituted the sacraments of the new law. There are seven: Baptism, Confirmation (or Chrismation), the Eucharist, Penance, the Anointing of the Sick, Holy Orders and Matrimony. The seven sacraments touch all the stages and all the important moments of Christian life: [64] they give birth and increase, healing and mission to the Christian's life of faith. There is thus a certain resemblance between the stages of natural life and the stages of the spiritual life." *Catechism, 1210*

C. *As Catholics We Believe...*

The Catechism groups the sacraments into three kinds: (1) The Sacraments of Initiation—Baptism, Confirmation, Eucharist; (2) The Sacraments of Healing—Reconciliation and Anointing of the Sick; (3) The Sacraments of Service to the Community—Holy Orders and Marriage.

The initiation sacraments move us toward the fullest incorporation into the Body of Christ. The healing sacraments bring us back to Christ and the Church when we have sinned and they prepare for our journey into death and beyond it to glory. The service to community sacraments strengthen the community life of the Church. Holy Orders provides the ordained ministers to serve the sanctification of the baptized members of the common priesthood of Christ, so they in turn may serve the sanctification of the world. Marriage serves the communal bonding of husband and wife and children and healthily serves the most critical unit of all society—the family.

*Sister
Benedicta (Edith) Stein*

Reflection

Edith Stein was born again in the sacrament of baptism. Edith Stein's entire life was characterized by an incessant search for truth and was illumined by the blessing of the Cross of Christ. She encountered the Cross for the first time in a deep faith of a widow of one of her university friends. The woman in mourning found strength and hope in the Cross of Christ. Later Edith wrote about this, "It was my first encounter with the Cross and the divine strength it gives to those who bear it. It was the moment my atheism collapsed. Christ shone so brightly! Christ in the mystery of the Cross!"

In My Life

1. When and where was I baptized? How do I celebrate my baptismal day? If I were to revisit the font where I was born in Christ, what kind of prayers and ceremonies would deepen my faith? Why would returning to the source of my life in Christ make my commitment to Jesus stronger today?

2. When and where was I confirmed? How old was I? What promises did I make then? How have I lived up to my confirmation pledges? How often am I willing to share my faith with others? What experiences have I had that made it painful for me to witness Jesus? What did I do in those challenging circumstances?

3. How easy is it for me to see the spiritual side of my sacramental life? What would help me appreciate the supernatural aspect of my reception of the sacraments? What is the connection of my moral life with my sacramental life?

"In him you also...were sealed with the promised holy Spirit...."

Ephesians 1:13

Prayer

Holy Father, Son and Spirit, I was baptized in your names and enriched with your blessings that delivered me from original and actual sins and filled with divine life as an adopted child of yours. I praise you for this and for the Holy Spirit's seal of Confirmation for the purpose of living a strong Christian life. May these sacraments continue to fill me with your divine abundance.

Glossary

Sacraments of Initiation—Baptism, Confirmation, Eucharist
Sacraments of Healing—Reconciliation and Anointing of Sick
Sacraments of Service to Community—Holy Orders and Marriage

Chapter 19

We Remember How You Loved Us

"Because the loaf of bread is one, we, though many, are one body, for we all partake of the one loaf."
I Corinthians 10:17

How Shall We Fully Revere This Wondrous Gift?

Jesus instituted the Eucharist at the Last Supper. While we have no explicit record of all that went on there, we can make a reasonable reconstruction based on our knowledge of Passover meals. When Jesus and apostles reclined on pillows on the floor around a low-rise table they saw on the table: (1) A roast lamb, portion of which had been sacrificed at the Temple. (2) A dish of endive, a bitter herb to remind them of the bitterness of Egyptian slavery. (3) Several plates of unleavened bread. (4) Dishes of a dip made of apples, dates, nuts and cinnamon which was both a flavoring and whose brick coloring reminded them of the bricks they were forced to make in Egypt. (5) Four cups of wine at each place setting.

Jesus opened the meal with a blessing, thanking the Father for all the blessings of creation and salvation. One of the apostles probably recited the story of the Exodus along with hymns of praise. Jesus took the first cup of wine and toasted the Father for his graces. Then Jesus took bread, blessed it and broke it. Normally he would have distributed the bread in silence, but he broke with tradition and said these words. "Take and eat. This is my Body, which will be given for you." The Bible remains silent about their thoughts and reactions at this point.

Now the meal began with the drinking of the second cup of wine. After the meal, Jesus took the third cup of wine and introduced with new words, "Take and drink. This is my blood which will be poured out for you." Again no record of their reaction is preserved. Then they lingered over the meal, talked and sang. The only time Jesus is reported as singing was here just before his death. At the conclusion of the Last Supper, Jesus went forth to his death and resurrection.

Is the Holy Eucharist more than a sacred meal?

A. *Some say...*
Since Jesus instituted the Eucharist at a meal and used eating and drinking language on the words of institution, it would seem that the Eucharist is a sacred meal. As in Biblical descriptions of the Breaking of the Bread, such as at Emmaus and the house liturgies described by Paul in *I Cor 10*. In *John 6* Jesus uses meal talk when he speaks of the Eucharist as the living bread.

And the most recorded miracle in the gospels (reported in all four gospels and twice in Mark) is the bread miracle, understood as a foreshadowing of the Eucharistic meal. The same is true of the wine miracle of Cana, equally a foreshadowing of the wine of the Eucharistic meal. Literature about the Eucharist frequently shows how it is connected to the Passover Meal, which becomes the true fulfillment of what the Passover was finally meant to be. Clearly the Eucharist is a sacred meal.

B. *The Catechism Teaches...*
...that the Eucharist is a sacrificial meal which makes present the saving cross and resurrection of Jesus in which we ultimately share in Communion.

"The Eucharist is the memorial of Christ's Passover, that is, the work of salvation accomplished by the life, death, and resurrection of Christ, a work made present by the liturgical action...."

"In an ancient prayer the Church acclaims the mystery of the Eucharist: 'O sacred banquet in which Christ is received as food, the memory of his Passion is renewed, the soul is filled with grace and a pledge of the life to come is given to us.'" [65] *Catechism, 1409, 1402*

The Eucharist is "the source and the summit of Christian life." (*Church, 11*) In the Eucharist is contained the entire treasure of the Church which is Jesus himself. All the sacraments and all the ministries of the Church flow toward and around the Eucharist. It is a sacrifice of praise, but also the sacrifice of Jesus made present for our salvation. It is as well the presence of the resurrection and the life which comes to us from the risen Jesus. It is a sacrificial meal in which we commune with Jesus himself and are renewed with grace and food for the journey of the apostolate.

We share in the benefits of Eucharist the more our inner selves are prepared for actively participating in the whole celebration: (1) The proclamation and homiletic explanation of the Word which calls us to faith and renewed covenant with Christ. (2) The Liturgy of the Sacrament, especially the "epiclesis" in which the Spirit is invoked to come and transform the bread and wine into the body and blood of Jesus, the words of institution, the great memorial prayers that follow. (3) The Communion with Jesus. We should ask Mary who prepared herself so profoundly for the reception of Jesus at the incarnation to prepare us for receiving Jesus in our hearts. We ought to be filled with praise and thanksgiving for the gift.

1. What does the Eucharistic celebration include?

"The Eucharistic celebration always includes: the proclamation of the Word of God; thanksgiving to God the Father for all his benefits, above all the gift of his Son; the consecration of the bread and wine; and participation in the liturgical banquet by receiving the Lord's body and blood. These elements constitute one single act of worship." *Catechism, 1408*

2. What happens at consecration in the Mass?

"By the consecration the transubstantiation of the bread and wine into the Body and Blood of Christ is brought about. Under the consecrated species of bread and wine Christ himself, living and glorious, is present in a true, real, and substantial manner: his Body and his Blood, with his soul and his divinity (cf. Council of Trent: DS 1640; 1651)." *Catechism, 1413*

3. How do we honor the Real Presence of Jesus in the tabernacle?

"Because Christ himself is present in the sacrament of the altar, he is to be honored with the worship of adoration. 'To visit the Blessed Sacrament is...a proof of gratitude, and expression of love, and a duty of adoration toward Christ our Lord.'" [66] (*Catechism, 1418*)

The priest raises the host during the Consecration.

C. As Catholics We Believe...

Several studies in recent years report that only one-third of Catholics have an adequate understanding of the conversion of the bread and wine into Christ's body and blood at Mass or when the host is received in Communion. Some think the host is only a symbol and Jesus is not really there. Others claim it is only when their faith says so that Jesus "then comes" alongside the host to which nothing has happened.

The Church continues, as always, to teach that the Holy Spirit comes and converts the bread and wine into Christ's body and blood, really and truly. The Spirit does this through the ministry of the ordained priest acting in the person of Christ. The value of Eucharistic devotions in times past, such as Eucharistic processions, Exposition of the Blessed Sacrament for public adoration, visits to the Blessed Sacrament, holy hours, silent thanksgiving after Communion, genuflecting before the tabernacles, keeping silent in Church—were all ways to be conscious of the truth of the Real Presence. Revival of these or comparable devotions would be valuable for the restoration of strong belief in Christ's Real Presence in the Eucharist.

Reflection

Scott Hahn, biblical scholar and convert to Catholicism from the Presbyterian church, has an interesting opinion about the fourth cup of wine at the Last Supper. He says the texts are not clear that Jesus drank it at the meal and in fact said that he would not drink that cup until he drank it with his disciples in the kingdom. Then Jesus went to Gethsemane where the angel presented Jesus with the "cup of suffering." Jesus prayed it would pass, but then accepted it as the Father's will.

At the Cross there were two wine presentations. The first one was a cup of soldier's wine, meant to reduce the pain of the crucified. Jesus refused this. In John's gospel, the second presentation takes place. Jesus had cried out, "I thirst." A soldier dipped a sponge in wine, put the sponge on a spear and raised it to Christ's lips. It is then Jesus looks at his whole life and suffering. All of it is completed. He has done the Father's will in every detail. Now he says, "It is finished." The "it" is the work of salvation from the aspect of suffering and the Cross. It is then Jesus "drinks" the "fourth cup" of wine—the fullness of suffering—from the sponge presented to him, for the kingdom's reality and presence is clearly about to burst upon the world in the resurrection soon to occur.

In My Life

1. What generally am I thinking of when I go to Holy Communion? How do I relate inwardly with Jesus at Communion? How clearly do I understand the real presence of Jesus in the transformed bread and wine I have received?

2. How do I renew my fervor and faith in my celebration of the Eucharist? What must I do to put more into the Mass so that I may "get more out of it?" How can I make the Eucharist the summit and source of my spirituality?

3. How could I help non-Catholics appreciate what I believe about the Holy Eucharist? As I look back on my life, what has been the history of my faith relation with Jesus in the Eucharist?

"The bread that we break, is it not a participation in the body of Christ?"

I Cor 10:16

Prayer

Eucharistic Lord, I believe in your real presence in the consecrated bread and wine. Help my unbelief. Holy Spirit, just as you transform the bread and wine into Christ's body and blood, transform my heart into perfect love for Jesus and others. Increase my faith in this most profound mystery of faith.

Glossary

Transubstantiation—The transforming of the substance of bread and wine into the substance of Christ's body and blood, soul and divinity, by the power of the Holy Spirit through the ministry of the ordained priest who acts in the person of Christ at Mass.

Chapter 20

The Healing Touch of Christ

*"As the Lord has forgiven you,
so must you also do."*

Colossians 3:13

My Brother, I Have Come To Pardon You.

In the Christmas season of 1983, *Time* magazine put a startling picture on its cover. It showed a prison cell. Two men sat on plastic chairs. One wore a white cassock, a white cape and a white skullcap. The other, a blue sweater, jeans and running shoes. *Time* reported the story this way:

"Last week in an extraordinary moment of grace, the violence in St. Peter's square was transformed. In a bare, white-walled cell in Rome's Rebbibia prison, John Paul tenderly held the hand that held the gun that was meant to kill him. For 21 minutes the pope sat with his would-be assassin, Mehmet Ali Agca. The two talked softly. Once or twice Agca laughed. The Pope forgave him for the shooting. At the end of the meeting, Agca either kissed the Pope's ring or pressed the Pope's hand to his forehead in a gesture of respect."

What did they talk about? "That," said the Pope as he left the cell, "will have to remain a secret between him and me. I spoke to him as a brother whom I have pardoned and who has my complete trust."

Did the Pope's visit influence Ali Agca? One year later Agca proclaimed that he was renouncing terrorism to become a man of peace. He traced his conversion to the Pope's visit with him a year ago. After extensive reading of the Koran, Agca said he had become a devout Muslim with profound respect for Christianity. He promised that if he were freed he would become a preacher to all nations proclaiming goodness and truth to all peoples.

Is revelation necessary?

A. *Some say...*
Forgiveness of sins occurs in the face of many practical difficulties. The Pope forgave Ali Agca. Does that mean Ali should be let out of prison? If a woman forgives the man who raped her, does this immediately dissolve the psychic pain and violation of self she experiences? Can we ask Israel to forgive the PLO terrorists who bombed and killed a busload of children?

How are the demands of justice met and the moral order maintained?

We say forgive and forget. But should Jews or any of us forget the holocaust? The "Balkan Ghosts and Irish Ghosts" of atrocities past linger in the present. To the present generation forgiveness seems like a betrayal of what was done to parents, grandparents and great-grandparents. Can genocide be forgiven?

The Sacrament of Reconciliation

B. *The Catechism Teaches...*
...that the sacraments of healing are first steps in a conversion process toward reconciliation and coping with the problem of pain.

The sacrament of Penance "is called the *sacrament of conversion* because it makes sacramentally present Jesus' call to conversion, the first step in returning to the Father[67] from whom one has strayed by sin."

"Illness and suffering have always been among the gravest problems confronted in human life."

"The first grace of [the sacrament of Anointing] is one of strengthening, peace and courage to overcome the difficulties that go with the condition of serious illness or the frailty of old age." *Catechism, 1423, 1500, 1520*

The sacraments of Reconciliation and Anointing initiate a process for dealing with the practical outcomes of divine healing in the face of evil and suffering. The Catechism regularly uses the expression "conversion" to refer to the lifelong process whereby our sacramental graces help us deal with the dilemmas caused by sin and pain in our lives.

When our hearts are open to the divine healing love that comes to us in these sacraments, we experience a basic inner transformation. In these sacraments God changes our hearts. With our converted hearts we have the confidence and the strength to take many steps, after the first one, to bring justice, morality and love to a wounded world. Just as there are many steps, so there are many "mini-conversions" offered by these sacraments as we grow stronger and deeper in our moral selves. We don't deny the practical problems, but we affirm that with God's help these mysteries of evil can be overcome.

1. Why do we need the sacrament of Reconciliation?

"The sinner wounds God's honor and love, his own human dignity...and the spiritual well-being of the Church...."

"The forgiveness of sins committed after Baptism is conferred by a particular sacrament called the sacrament of conversion, confession, penance, or reconciliation." *Catechism, 1487, 1486*

2. What are the elements of the sacrament of Penance?

"The sacrament of Penance is a whole consisting in three actions of the penitent and the priest's absolution. The penitent's acts are repentance, confession or disclosure of sins to the priest, and the intention to make reparation and do works of reparation." *Catechism, 1491*

3. What is the sacrament of Anointing?

"The sacrament of Anointing of the Sick has as its purpose the conferral of a special grace on the Christian experiencing the difficulties inherent in the condition of grave illness or old age."

"This assistance from the Lord by the power of his Spirit is meant to lead the sick person to healing of the soul, but also of the body if such is God's will.[68] Furthermore, 'if he has committed sins, he will be forgiven.'" [69] *Catechism, 1527, 1520*

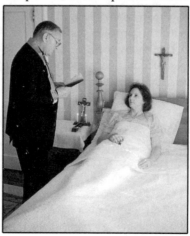

Anointing of the Sick

C. As Catholics We Believe...

We believe that God uses water of the Spirit to baptize us and change us into adopted sons and daughters of the Father. Our faith teaches us that the Spirit changes bread and wine into the saving body and blood of Jesus. We should also have great confidence in the transforming powers of the sacraments of healing—Reconciliation and Anointing. God then uses our gestures of healing as part of the conversion process. Our extended and humble hands of forgiveness and love make channels of grace, in the Spirit, for those whom we touch. Forgiveness is not a useless passion, nor does it ignore the practical problems which it faces. But it is the beginning, the first step to healing a wounded world and raising the curtain—though ever so slightly—on the solution to the mystery of pain, suffering and death.

Reflection

In 1993, Katherine Ann Power surrendered and acknowledged her role in a 1970 bank robbery in which Officer Walter Schroeder was fatally shot. The nephew of the slain officer was interviewed. He said that he was very angry at the time of the murder. He would have easily called for her to be put up against a wall and shot. He would have taken her to his aunt's home and showed her what she did to those nine children.

Years later, the nephew finds himself forgiving Ms. Power. He said that for 49 years he was taught to forgive by his father and his Church. This lesson gets more deeply imbedded with the years. "We have a very short life to live. There's no use hating people. I want my children to forgive."

In My Life

1. What stories can I share about forgiveness problems in myself and my family? Why does forgiveness delayed for many years become forgiveness denied? What are three excuses I have used to refuse forgiveness?

2. How would I speak of forgiveness to a woman raped, a man mugged, a child abused? Why does the Church teach that the sacraments of healing (Reconciliation and Anointing of the Sick) are but "first steps" in a conversion process that leads to healing?

3. When I hear of people having cancer, of burying a dead relative or friend, of suffering psychological traumas, how do I react to these problems of pain and death? What light does the sacrament of Anointing shed on the problem of pain?

"Is anyone among you suffering?... He should summon the presbyters of the church, and they should pray over him and anoint [him] with oil in the name of the Lord...."

James 5:13-14

Prayer

Have mercy upon me, O Lord and forgive me my sins. Transform my heart with your Holy Spirit of conversion that I may be a witness of healing to my family, my friends and the world. Give me an understanding heart in the face of the pain and death.

Glossary

Conversion—Powered by the Spirit, this is a lifelong process of inner change so we may be a witness of light in a world dark with hate, pain and death.

Chapter 21

The Sacred Acts of Marriage

"I will espouse you to me forever...."
Hosea 2:21

Why, It's a Lion I've Married! A Lion!

St. Thomas More

Catholic Church history remembers the story of a husband who loved his wife and children dearly. In fact this man went to his death rather than approve of a king who wanted to divorce his wife. The man was St. Thomas More. The king was England's Henry VIII. The king put Thomas in the Tower of London with the intention of executing him unless he approved of the divorce. Thomas had been his chancellor, one of the best known men in England and admired for his moral character. The king craved his approval.

More's opposition left his family impoverished. Hence the Prime Minister was able to persuade his wife Alice, his daughter Margaret and her husband Roper to go to the Tower and urge More to change his mind. Their arguments failed. Thomas would not bend on the matter of fidelity in marriage.

As dramatized by Robert Bolt in *A Man For All Seasons*, More eats a lunch Alice has prepared for him and compliments her on the tastiness of her custard and the stylishness of her dress. She rebukes him for such inconsequential remarks at so serious a moment. He accepts her correction and begs her to understand why he must remain faithful to his convictions. He tells her he cannot make a "good death" until she tries to understand why he is doing this.

Alice says she does not understand. She wounds him by saying that his death will be no good to her. She fears that after he dies she will hate him for what he has done. More breaks down and reveals his loneliness and pain that touches the very heart of their marriage. "You mustn't, you—."

It is then that Alice responds to him from her heart and not her fears. She rushes to him, hugs him tightly and confesses, "S-s-sh...As for understanding, I understand you're the best man I've ever met or am likely to." Then she roars at the prison walls that if the king or the council want to know what she thinks of them, they have only to ask her.

More's face shines with joy as he rocks his wife back and forth and declares, "Why, it's a lion I married! A lion!"

Heart has met heart.

Is marriage for spousal love or for children?

A. *Some say...*

It would seem that the main purpose of marriage is for nurturing the love of husband and wife. The Bible refers to this when God created marriage in the first place. "That is why a man leaves his father and mother and clings to his wife, and the two of them become one body." *(Gn 2:24)*

In commenting on the sacrament of Marriage, Vatican II says, "Our Savior...encounters Christian spouses through the sacrament of marriage. He abides with them in order that by their mutual self-giving spouses will love each other with enduring fidelity, as he loved the Church and delivered himself for it.[70] Authentic married love is caught up into divine love and is directed and enriched by the redemptive power of Christ...." *(Modern World, 48)*

The primary importance of spousal love is demonstrated in this little story. Some years ago in London, Sir Winston Churchill and his wife, Lady Clementine attended a dinner in their honor. During the meal the guests played a game, "If you couldn't be who you are, who would you like to be?"

Various replies were heard. But all wondered how Sir Winston would answer. Surely he would not want to be a Caesar or a Bonaparte. He arose as the last speaker. "If I can't be who I am, I would most like to be"— the 78-year-old turned to his wife and took her hand—"Lady Churchill's second husband."

The Catechism Teaches...

B. ...that the principal purposes of marriage are the loving union of spouses in Christ, openness to fertility and the full nurturing of their children for the good of the family, the church and society.

"'God himself is the author of marriage.'[71] ...Marriage is not a purely human institution despite the many variations it may have undergone through the centuries in different cultures, social structures, and spiritual attitudes.... 'The well being of the individual person and of both human and Christian society is closely bound up with the healthy state of conjugal and family life.'"[72] *Catechism, 1603*

God created us out of love and calls us to love, being in his image and likeness. God intended this love to be fruitful. "'Be fertile and multiply; fill the earth and subdue it.'" *(Gn 1:28)* The loving union of the spouses is threatened by sin—discord, infidelity, jealousy and a spirit of domination. This can escalate into hatred and separation. Hence the spouses need the abundant graces of God that are designed to heal the sin that strikes at the heart of marriage.

The sacrament of Matrimony is filled with these graces of healing and renewal for the spouses. The sacrament perfects the couples' love, strengthens their indissoluble unity and helps them to attain holiness, happiness, fulfillment and profound resources of love for nurturing their children. Jesus is the source of this grace. Jesus encounters the Christian spouses in the sacrament of Marriage, gives them the strength to take up the crosses and challenges, to rise again from falls, to forgive one another, to bear one another's burdens and to love one another with tender, fruitful and supernatural love.

1. What does the sacrament of Marriage signify?

"The sacrament of Matrimony signifies the union of Christ and the Church. It gives spouses the grace to love each other with the love with which Christ has loved his Church; the grace of the sacrament thus perfects the human love of the spouses, strengthens their indissoluble unity and sanctifies them on the way to eternal life (cf. Council of Trent: DS 1799)." *Catechism, 1661*

2. What are the "goods" of marriage?

(1) "The love of the spouses requires, of its very nature, the unity and indissolubility of the spouses' community of persons, which embraces their entire life.... This human communion is confirmed, purified, and completed by communion Jesus Christ, given through the sacrament of Matrimony."

(2) "By its very nature conjugal love requires the inviolable fidelity of the spouses."

(3) "By its very nature the institution of marriage and married

love is ordered to the procreation and education of the offspring and it is in them that it finds its crowning glory."[73] *Catechism, 1644, 1646, 1652*

3. What is the importance of the Christian home?

"The Christian home is the place where children receive the first proclamation of the faith. For this reason the family home is rightfully called 'the domestic church,' a community of grace and prayer, a school of human virtues and of Christian charity." *Catechism, 1666*

The Sacrament of Holy Matrimony

Reflection

"How can I ever express the happiness of a marriage joined by the Church, strengthened by an offering, sealed by a blessing, announced by angels and ratified by the Father?...How wonderful the bond between two believers, now one in hope, one in desire, one in discipline, one in the same service! They are both children of one Father and servants of the same Master, undivided in spirit and flesh, truly two in one flesh. Where the flesh is one, one also is the spirit." (Tertullian, "To a Wife," 2, 8, 6-7)

In My Life

1. When I look at couples and families I admire, what are the reasons for my good impressions? As I observe couples who have a strong fidelity to one another, what appears to me to be the secret of their abiding love? Whenever I think of the marriage ideals what comes to my mind?

2. Why is religion and the sacrament of Matrimony such a resource of strength to wedded people? What are the standards parents should follow in properly nurturing, educating and raising their children? What happens to the children of irresponsible parents?

3. When I meet faithfully committed virgins and celibates what do I perceive to be the backbone of their witness? How do I (should I) treat adult singles who, either from choice or circumstances, will probably not marry?

"There was a wedding in Cana in Galilee, and the mother of Jesus was there. Jesus and his disciples were also invited to the wedding."

Jn 2:1-2

Prayer

Jesus, by your presence at the wedding feast of Cana, you taught us that you are the third "member of a Christian sacramental wedding." I pray that your grace-filled presence to all sacramentally married couples will be a source of love, unity and fidelity for them. I pray also for your blessings on vowed virgins and celibates as well as dedicated single people.

Glossary

The "Goods" of Marriage—The goods and requirements of Christian marriage are: (1) Unity and Indissolubility (2) Fidelity of conjugal love (3) Openness to fertility.

Chapter 22

The Beauty of the Catholic Priesthood

"Do this in memory of me...."
"Father...consecrate them in the truth."
Luke 22:19; John 17:17

Nazi Guard: "Who are you?"
Father Kolbe: "I am a Catholic Priest"

Father Kolbe as he looked during the early days of his imprisonment at Auschwitz

Auschwitz death camp, 1941.

A siren sounded announcing that a prisoner had escaped. The guards convened the inmates. The commander informed them that ten of them would be selected for starvation as a reprisal for the escapee. Slowly and deliberately he passed through row after row and eventually designated the ten victims.

One of the chosen, Francis Gajowniczek, wept openly and cried out, "My wife and my children!"

Suddenly a prisoner broke ranks. It was Father Maximilian Kolbe. With a firm step he walked calmly to the front of the assembly. "I want to speak to the commander." "What do you want," asked commander Fritsch. Pointing to the sobbing man, Kolbe replied, "I want to die in place of this prisoner. I have no wife or children. Besides I'm old and not good for anything. He's in better condition."

"Who are you?"

"I'm a Catholic priest."

"Request granted."

Kolbe and the nine others were taken to basement cells in the death block, stripped and left to starve. "You'll dry up like tulips," said the guard. Kolbe encouraged the men. "Hold on, the escapee may be found." He led them in prayer. After two weeks only four were still alive, Kolbe among them. A doctor came and injected each of them with carbolic acid. Death came in less than a minute. It was the evening before the feast of the Assumption.

As a young man, Kolbe had written to his mother, "I pray that I may love without limits." God heard his prayer. And what happened to the man he saved? He survived Auschwitz and attended the ceremony in which Pope John Paul II canonized St. Maximilian Kolbe in St. Peter's basilica in 1982.

Is the ordained priesthood the same as the common priesthood of all the faithful?

A. **Some say...**

...it would seem that the ordained priest is simply a special function of the baptismal priesthood received by every Catholic. The ordained priest is chosen from among the members of the congregation to represent them at the altar before God. At the ordination ceremony the people's recommendation is sought. The bishop says, "Do you find him worthy?" The respondent says, "*After inquiry among the people of Christ* and the recommendation of those concerned with his training, I testify that he has been found worthy." The assembly acknowledges the selection of the ordinand by applause. The whole Church is a priestly people. The ordained priest has special duties in the Church.

B. **The Catechism Teaches...**

...that the ordained priest differs in essence and not just in degree (more than a priest) from the baptismal priesthood.

"The ministerial priesthood differs in essence from the common priesthood of the faithful because it confers a sacred power for the service of the faithful. The ordained ministers exercise their service for the People of God by teaching *(munus docendi)*, divine worship *(munus liturgicum)* and pastoral governance *(munus regendi)*." *Catechism, 1592*

In the sacrament of Holy Orders the priest is ordained to serve the sanctification of the People of God, through the power of the Spirit. In the sacrament of Baptism the People of God are initiated into the common priesthood of all the faithful for the purpose of sanctifying the world with God's grace.

The priest is expected to be a shepherd, humbly serving the Body of Christ. In this he should bond people to the Church as a divine mystery of salvation. He must build up a community of faith and maintain the institution of the Church for the sake of stability, continuity and service.

The priest is expected to be a minister of the Word, proclaiming and witnessing the Gospel of salvation. He also is a minister of the Sacraments of Eucharist and Reconciliation. At Eucharist he acts "in the person of Christ" so that the mystery of salvation is made present and offered to the Father on behalf of God's People.

1. What are the Holy Orders?

"Since the beginning, the ordained ministry has been conferred and exercised in three degrees: that of bishops, that of presbyters [priests], and that of deacons...."

The bishop receives the fullness of the sacrament of Holy Orders, which integrates him into the episcopal college and makes him the visible head of the particular Church entrusted to him. As successors of the apostles and members of the college, the bishops share in the apostolic responsibility and mission of the whole Church under the authority of the Pope, successor of St. Peter." *Catechism, 1593-1594*

2. What is the role of presbyters (priests)?

"Priests are united with the bishops in sacerdotal dignity and at the same time depend on them in the exercise of their pastoral functions; they are called to be the bishops' prudent co-workers. They form around their bishop the presbyterium which bears responsibility with him for the particular Church. They receive from the bishop the charge of a parish community or a determinate ecclesial office." *Catechism, 1595*

3. What is the role of deacons?

"Deacons are ministers ordained for tasks of service of the Church; they do not receive the ministerial priesthood, but ordination confers on them important functions in the ministry of the word, divine worship, pastoral governance, and the service of charity, tasks which they must carry out under the pastoral authority of their bishop." *Catechism, 1596*

C. As Catholics We Believe...

Priests are ordained to teach, preach, explain and defend the Word of God within the tradition of the Church. Their effectiveness in this ministry of the Word is essentially related to their personal lives which must witness what is proclaimed. Priests are also ordained to celebrate the Eucharist which is the summit and source of the Christian life and contains the entire treasury of the Church, Jesus himself. *(Cf. Priests, 5)* In addition, priests are ordained to hear confessions and in the name of God offer absolution from sins. Priests should teach people to pray, help them to become a living community of faith, serve, protect and defend the poor from injustice and exploitation. To do this effectively priests must have a strong relationship to Jesus who brings them to the Father in the Spirit. They must be men of prayer, profound spirituality and humbly aware of their human frailty.

The Sacrament of Holy Orders

Reflection

A few years ago, Father Francis Giliberti, pastor of a poor parish in Philadelphia, won a million dollar jackpot at Atlantic City. When asked what he would do with the money, he said, "I am giving it to charity. I don't need the money. I have found all the fulfillment I ever wanted in being a priest."

In 1961, Msgr. William Nolan founded Aquinas House at Dartmouth College as a Catholic Center for the students. He presided there for 25 years. During that time, he served the countless needs of thousands of students. He also inspired the vocations of 45 priests, 1 bishop and 3 nuns. When asked what his secret was, he said, "I must be a happy priest. I am not an academic nor a secular sophisticate. I know I must try to preach a good sermon, often a long one, always full of doctrine. I am obliged to be a man of prayer."

In My Life

1. How aware am I that I have a "calling" from God, consistent with his gifts and talents to me, to a certain way of life? I may be called to the priesthood or religious life, or to the married vocation or to that of being a dedicated single person. What do I see about myself in regard to these options?

2. Who are some priests and religious men and women that have been good friends to me and who have been an inspiration to me? If I sense that God is calling me to priesthood or religious life, what am I doing about it? What should I be doing? What would my parents think about such a calling?

3. What are the kinds of service to the world that I could exercise effectively as a priest or religious? How strong is my prayer life? How do I pass each day in conscious but quiet service to others?

"You are a priest forever...."

Hebrews 5:6

Prayer

Heavenly Father, I praise you for the high priesthood of your Son, Jesus Christ, and for all our bishops and priests who share in this ministerial priesthood. I also praise you for the service received from our deacons and all members of the religious life. I ask that I may be open to the call to priesthood or religious life should that be your holy will.

Glossary

Presbyter—Another name for priest.

Presbyterate—Name given to the community of priests in a given diocese or archdiocese.

Monsignor—Honorary title given to a priest for singular service to the Church.

Cardinal—Honorary title given to a bishop or archbishop for a variety of reasons. Cardinals, under 80, alone may elect a pope.

Chapter 23

Building Blocks for the Catholic Moral Life

"If you wish to enter into life,
keep the commandments."
Matthew 19:17

O Father, Peace!
For the Love of God!

The strong hand of God touched Catherine of Siena from the earliest days of her childhood (1347-1380). She felt the powerful attraction of divine love and responded to it. By the time she was a teenager she was advancing in prayer and active in good works. She was involved in prison ministry, especially to those on death row. She volunteered long hours at the hospital and alleviated the needs of the poor.

Graced as a mystic by the Holy Spirit, she sought to be a nun but was refused. She became a lay associate of the Dominican Sisters. In young womanhood she attracted numerous disciples who came to her for guidance in prayer. Kings wrote to her for moral advice on political matters.

A major Church problem of the late fourteenth century was the "Avignon Papacy." Years before Catherine, the popes had moved from Rome to Avignon. Unhappily the French monarchy exercised too much control over the papacy. Worse yet, a spirit of avarice and corruption affected the papal court. The City-State of Florence asked Catherine to go to Avignon to settle a war between them and the papal forces.

Catherine accepted the challenge. Her goals were to bring peace and to persuade Gregory XI to go back to Rome. She arrived alone with no other forces than her faith, prayer and trust in God. For three months, despite opposition from Cardinals and the nobility with vested interests, she went every day to see the pope and argue the cause for peace and the reform of the Church.

"Be a man, Father! Begin the reform of the Church through appointing worthy priests. Make peace in Italy, not with the sword but with mercy and the Cross." She used a thousand ways to change the pope's mind and urge him back to Rome. Her 90-day crusade finally prevailed. She had the joy of escorting the pope to a ship that conveyed him and his cardinals back to Rome. Her moral backbone—backed up by faith and prayer—began this process of Church renewal. She died at the age of 33, reproaching herself that she had not loved Jesus enough. The Church canonized her in 1461 and made her co-patroness of Italy, along with St. Francis of Assisi, in 1939.

St. Catherine of Siena

Does not love of God eliminate the need for commandments?

A. *Some say...*
It would appear that loving God is all we need. Love would then overcome the need for commandments. For lovers the love is enough. After all, Augustine said, "Love God and do what you will." When Jesus was asked what the greatest commandments were, he spoke of love, the love of God, others and self. So, if there is to be any commandments that we should pay attention to, it would be the commands about love.

Love seems to be all we need. We all know of people who follow the rules of religion and brag about how well they observe the commandments. Yet they often seem to be harsh people, lacking love. They substitute observance for love. Conversely, love seems sufficient, for lovers will always know how to act due to their sensitivity to the beloved.

B. *The Catechism Teaches...*

...that the moral life begins with a love covenant with God, but also embraces the commandments which spell out the meaning and consequences of love.

"When someone asks him [Jesus], 'Which commandment in the Law is the greatest?' [74] Jesus replies, 'You shall love the Lord, your God with all your heart, and with all your soul, and with all your mind. This is the greatest and first commandment. And a second is like it: You shall love your neighbor as yourself....' [75] The Decalogue must be interpreted in the light of this twofold yet single commandment of love, the fullness of Law...." *Catechism, 2055*

At Mount Sinai, God enters into a covenant of love with Israel before giving them the ten commandments. Morality is rooted in a relationship with God. We fall in love with God in covenant. Commandments show us how to stay in love with God. Christ's citation of the laws of love says the same thing. The Catechism entitles its beginning section on morality, "Life in the Spirit," to indicate the essential role of covenant love. But the Catechism will go on to discuss the role of the commandments.

But there is more to morality than covenant and commandments. We need the beatitudes to remind us that the quest for happiness is a powerful motivation to be moral, for only the moral life can make us truly happy. We need to acquire virtues so that we will develop good habits that make it easier for us to love and keep the commandments. We need the seven gifts of the Holy Spirit as graces both to acquire the virtues and to do what is right. We need to become conscious of the reality of sin, both original and actual, so we know the origin and reality of evil, what to avoid as well as what to practice positively in its place.

1. What constitutes our human dignity and why does it contribute to our moral life?

"The dignity of the human person is rooted in his creation in the image and likeness of God...; it is fulfilled in his vocation to divine beatitude.... It is essential to a human being freely to direct himself to this fulfillment...; By his deliberate actions...the human person does, or does not, conform to the good promised by God and attested by moral conscience.... Human beings make their own contribution to their interior growth; they make their whole sentient and spiritual lives into means of this growth.... With the help of grace they grow in virtue..., avoid sin, and if they sin they entrust themselves as did the prodigal son[76] to the mercy of our Father in heaven.... In this way they attain to the perfection of charity. *Catechism, 1700*

2. What is sin?

"Sin is an offense against reason, truth, and right conscience; it is failure in genuine love for God and neighbor caused by a perverse attachment to certain goods...."

"Sin sets itself against God's love for us and turns our hearts away from it." *Catechism, 1849-1850 (For* Original Sin*, Cf. 416-417)*

3. What is the role of grace?

"The grace of the Holy Spirit has the power to justify us, that is, to cleanse us from our sins and to communicate to us 'the righteousness of God through faith in Jesus Christ' and through Baptism."[77] *Catechism, 1987*

C. *As Catholics We Believe...*

Let your conscience be your guide. This is good Catholic teaching so long as we understand that our consciences must be informed and formed. What helps us form our consciences. (1) Natural Law. This refers to the fact that God gave us a reason that can tell the difference between good and bad. Natural law is a reflection of the divine law in our hearts. (2) The Ten Commandments. These are concrete applications of natural law. Because sin has darkened our minds and emotions, God gave us these commandments in the revelation to Moses. (3) The Teachings of Jesus. Christ's Sermon on the Mount *(Mt 5-7)* outlines the fundamentals of his moral teachings. His Last Supper Discourse *(Jn 13-17)* shows how love, divine adoption and our relation to the Trinity serve as both the motivation to be moral and how we receive the grace to be good.

(4) The Teachings of the Church. The Magisterium (our Spirit-guided Church as teacher) applies the natural law, the covenant and commandments and the teachings of Jesus to new moral questions as they have arisen in Church history. (5) The Holy Spirit at work in us. The Spirit convinces us of our sinfulness, convicts us of it, converts us from sin and consoles us in the process. This is the broad outline of how we go about forming our consciences. Other elements should be considered, but these are the starting points.

Reflection

"The ten commandments, which should always flow from covenant love of God, others, self, are a two-edged sword. One side of each commandment illustrates a virtue to be acquired. The other side forbids a specific behavior. Both should be considered when examining the commandments. Here is an outline of what is meant:

Virtue to be Acquired	Sin to be Avoided
1. Faith in a real God	Idolatry of self or world
2. Reverence for God, others	Blasphemy, Secularism
3. Worship, dependence on God	False pride, self salvation
4. Family values	Irresponsibility, disobedience
5. Sacredness of life	Murder, terrorism, abortion, etc.
6. Marital fidelity	Adultery, fornication, etc.
7. Justice, individual/social	Injustice, stealing, etc.
8. Truthfulness, honesty	Lies, betrayal
9. Chastity	Lust
10. Generosity	Avarice

"If you wish to be perfect, go, sell what you have and give to [the] poor.... Then come, follow me."

Mt 19:21

Prayer

Jesus, you are our greatest moral teacher and the outstanding exemplar of this teaching. I pray that I may learn your teaching and receive the graces to form my conscience correctly so I may live in covenant with you and keep the commandments as a sign of my covenant commitment.

Glossary

Covenant—A grace filled bonding between us and God.

Wounds of Original Sin—Effects of original sin in us even after baptism: (1) Weakness in our will to do the good (2) Disorder in our passions (3) Malice in our minds (4) Ignorance, which makes it hard for us to know truth and be honest about ourselves.

Chapter 24

My Soul Thirsts for the Living God

The First Commandment
"O God, you are my God whom I seek;
for you my flesh pines and my soul thirsts
like the earth, parched, lifeless and without water."
Psalm 63:2

C. S. Lewis—Surprised By God

C. S. Lewis, one of the 20th century's towering religious writers, was born a Protestant in Ulster, Ireland. As a child he was taught to say his prayers and taken to church, but he said he was not especially interested. His mother died of cancer when he was nine. His father became withdrawn, leaving Lewis and his brother to fend for themselves.

In his early teens he was sent to England to an Anglo-Catholic boarding school. The boys were taken to church twice every Sunday. Lewis began seriously to pray, read the Bible and obey his conscience. His religious fervor did not last. He went on to be tutored in preparation for Oxford. His tutor trained him rigorously in logic. Lewis meanwhile abandoned religion.

What eventually led him back to God? Lewis wrote about this in his book, *Surprised By Joy*. It was "joy" that drew him to God. What was this joy? It was a series of fleeting experiences, over a number of years, that came to him unexpectedly—from a poem, a memory, a scene. It felt like the mystery of life suddenly opened a door for him briefly and then closed again.

Joy left him with an inner longing for "something or someone."

It was painful because he knew he didn't have it. It was pleasurable because he knew he could.

And then one night when he was a student at Magdalen College, Oxford, God possessed him. "You must picture me alone in that room at Magdalene, feeling...the steady, unrelenting approach of Him whom I desired earnestly not to meet...In the Trinity term of 1929 I gave in, and admitted that God was God, and knelt and prayed:

perhaps, that night, the most dejected and reluctant convert in all England." (*Surprised by Joy* London: Collins, Fontana Books, 1959, pages 182-183)

Lewis eventually became a committed Christian and devoted his enormous literary talent to a number of persuasive, often humorous, common sense, yet faith-filled books about Christianity. His works sell a million copies a year. Through his writings, he has probably made more converts to Christianity than anyone else in the 20th century. His soul thirsted for God. And God came to him.

Is it better to use reason or faith to draw people to God?

A. **Some say...**
The first Vatican Council said that we can come to know God's existence from using our reason. The Second Vatican Council teaches that God has put within us a deep inner longing for God. If we pay attention to this inner hunger, this can lead us to God. It would seem that for our age this approach is best. While some could reason their way to God, most people would probably have a better chance of discovering God by becoming aware of their inner longings.

The psalms appear to say the same. "Athirst is my soul for God, the living God." *(Ps 42:3)* St. Augustine claims his conversion was a combination of experiencing an inner drive to a "someone" along with God trying to break into his awareness, "shouting at him and piercing his deafness." Other converts testify they felt an emptiness which they discovered only God could fill.

B. **The Catechism Teaches...**
...that God gives us three ways to reach him—by reason, by nourishing our inner longing for the infinite, by faith in his revelation.

"With his openness to truth and beauty, his sense of moral goodness, his freedom and the voice of his conscience, with his longings for the infinite and for happiness, man questions himself about God's existence. In all this he discerns signs of his spiritual soul." *Catechism, 33*

While reason and our inner longings are ways to know the real God, we are given God's revelation of himself, his love and his inner life so that we can, with assurance and conviction come to him in faith. This is the gift of God enunciated in the first commandment. God lovingly invites us to "believe in a real God." If our reason falters or our inattentiveness to our inner hunger fails us, we still have a yet richer gift for discovering the beauty and the wonder of God. To make this faith grow we are also endowed with gifts of hope, love, prayer, adoration and social responsibility. When we accept these gifts we also agree to live them with energy, enthusiasm and joy.

Our world is confused about this truth. Hence many are yet atheists, agnostics, irreligious or trusting in magic, astrology or other substitutes for a real God. Many make a god of self, money or sex. These are all self defeating and self destructive behaviors that rob people of joy, hope and salvation.

1. What does the first commandment invite us to do?

"The first commandment summons man to believe in God, to hope in him, and to love him above all else."

"God has loved us first. The love of the One God is recalled in the first of the 'ten words [commandments].' The commandments then make explicit the response of love that man is called to give to his God." *Catechism, 2134, 2083*

2. How does this commandment relate to the moral life?

"Our moral life has its source in faith in God who reveals his love to us. St. Paul speaks of the 'obedience of faith'[78] as our first obligation. He shows that 'ignorance of God' is the principle and explanation of all moral deviations.[79] Our duty toward God is to believe in him and to bear witness to him." *Catechism,* 2087

3. What is the "idolatry" that this commandment forbids?

"Human life finds its unity in the adoration of the one God. The commandment to worship the Lord alone integrates man and saves him from an endless disintegration. Idolatry is a perversion of man's innate religious sense. An idolater is someone who 'transfers his indestructible notion of God to anything other than God.'"[80] *Catechism, 2114*

C. *As Catholics We Believe...*

The culture in which we proclaim the first commandment's invitation to faith in a real God urges us rather to doubt, skepticism and cynicism. These are illusions that both deny our real nature and the possibilities of joy for which we long. The Catechism calls us to faith that makes us "confident and convinced" believers in God and disciples of Jesus. Confidence! Conviction! Those are the attitudes that will fulfill us, because they have a true, infinite, all loving God as the focus.

What is faith? "Faith is the *assurance* of things hoped for, the *conviction* of things not seen." (*Heb* 11:1, RSV Tr.; italics mine) The world is full of uncertain trumpets, competing ideologies and weary with searching without finding, of questioning but hearing no answers. The first commandment calls us to faith in God so we can live with a blessed assurance in the reality of God and glorious conviction that we are loved and saved by God.

Reflection

C.S. Lewis went to his knees before God who touched him in his rooms at Magdalen in the Trinity term of 1939. He still needed faith in Jesus as Son of God and redeemer. He began studying the Bible and the theology of redemption. The miracle of grace occurred for him during a visit to a zoo. "When I set out I did not believe that Jesus Christ is the Son of God, and when we reached the zoo, I did. Yet I had not exactly spent the journey in thought. Nor in great emotion. 'Emotional' is perhaps the last word we can apply to some of the most important events. It was more like when a man, after a long sleep, still lying motionless in bed, becomes aware that he is now awake." (Surprised by Joy, p. 189)

In My life

1. What are occasions in my life when I have felt "religious," or had an experience of God's presence? What effect did that have on my prayer life and moral behavior? What similar experiences have I heard or read about from other people ?

2. When faced with doubt, skepticism and cynicism about religion and God's existence and love, what is my response? What impact does the New Testament teaching about faith as assurance and conviction about God have on me? What is the difference between an assured and convinced Catholic and a timid and doubtful one?

3. What would I do to help unbelievers come to faith in God? How would I react if, after my best and enduring efforts, the unbeliever still did not believe? How would I react if my efforts to convert an unbeliever succeeded?

"I will give thanks to you, O LORD, with all my heart...."

Ps 138:1

Prayer

I believe in God and in you, Lord Jesus. Help my unbelief. Show me how to walk by faith. Replace my doubts with faith. Turn my skepticism into blessed assurance in the truth of your love. Remove the cynicism from my mind so I am filled with graced conviction in your glorious gift of redemption.

Glossary

First Commandment— "I, the LORD, am your God....You shall not have other gods besides me." *Dt 5:6-7*

Idolatry—Any behavior that attributes to self, money, sex or anything else that which belongs only to God.

Chapter 25

Rediscover the Sacred

The Second Commandment
"The place where you stand is holy ground."

Exodus 3:5

An Angel Touched Him
With God's Holiness

*The Prophet
Isaiah*

One of the Bible's greatest prophets is Isaiah. Born about 762 BC, he grew up in a family that taught him reverence for God, a feeling for the sacred in the midst of life and a passion for justice. His parents taught him how wrong it was for the rich to oppress the poor. They held family discussions about the prevalence of bribery at the king's court. They sang the psalms together and worshiped at the Temple. Isaiah's father and mother gave him a religious and moral conscience.

On his 21st birthday, Isaiah received an invitation to the coronation of King Jotham. The ceremony engulfed him—the music of the psalms, the smell of incense, the royal procession, the colorful robes of the celebrants, the splendid stage of the Temple inside of which was the "Holy of Holies" where God dwelt with his people.

Suddenly this grand physical reality was transposed into a spiritual one. (Read *Isaiah 6*) Isaiah had an unexpected religious experience. Jotham's throne became God's throne. Angels' songs replaced the earthly singers. The gold angels on the ark became live ones, seraphim, which means "fiery angels." The rich robes became God's garments. Isaiah felt God's closeness, like cloth against the skin. The incense became the *shekinah*, a word for cloud, the shining cloud of God's glory.

As he experienced the living presence of God, he heard the angels sing of God's holiness. The scene filled Isaiah with inexpressible joy, a sense of the purity of God and an unforgettable realization of the presence of the sacred. Awe enveloped him. Then the scene faded for a moment. Isaiah turned back to himself and felt the difference between himself and what he had just seen. How "secular" he was. How "sacred and beautiful" is God. He longed to be closer to God.

The scene returned and an angel came and touched him with a burning coal that symbolized the holiness of God. He heard God say that he wanted a missionary to bring justice and a sense of the sacred to his people. "Who will do this for me?" Filled with gratitude to God, Isaiah answered, "Here I am, Lord. Send me on this mission."

Is not the modern preoccupation with the secular the best way to acquire a sense of the sacred?

A. *Some say...*
Secular wisdom, seemingly, has a great deal to teach us. Freedom, democracy, human rights, mutual respect, tolerance for others' views are values we all admire. Secular science and medicine have performed miracles of health and comfort unknown in previous ages. Experts seem able to explain everything about the surfaces of things, the objective world.

The modernized nations in Western Europe, North America, the Pacific rim, Australia and New Zealand are showcases for what secular wisdom has been able to achieve. Is it not reasonable to say there is something "sacred" about all this? Is not this "secular city" a kind of "new Jerusalem," God's kingdom on earth?

The Catechism Teaches...

B. ...that the Sacred is God's presence and action in the midst of life and that a specific and disciplined attention is necessary to become aware of the Sacred.

"The sense of the sacred is part of the virtue of religion. 'Are these feelings of fear and awe Christian feelings or not?...They are the feelings we *should* have—yes, have to an intense degree—if we literally had sight of almighty God. They are the feelings we shall have, *if* we realize His presence. In proportion as we believe that He is present, we shall have them; and not to have them, is not to realize, not to believe that He is present.'" *(Cardinal Newman, "Parochial and Plain Sermons," Vol. 2, 21-22)*

The second commandment invites us to be aware of God's presence in the midst of our daily lives. This is another way of saying we ought to be conscious of the sacred and the holy in creation and in each person we meet. Only our faith in this possibility opens us up to this presence of God among us. When we experience God's holiness in creation and persons, then we reverence both the God who is present and the gifts of the world and human persons. Put plainly, when we reverence God, we will reverence people and the environment.

When we have awe for God's glory, we will have awe for people and things and honor their integrity and dignity. And we will have the respect for our own bodies and souls that we hunger for. Our self worth is rooted in God. Our self respect comes from an awareness that God loves us and even at this moment is providentially keeping us in existence.

The second commandment says we shall not make wrong use of God's name. Biblically the word "name" refers to the essence and existence of the person. To say someone's name with scorn is to dishonor the person. That is why cursing and blasphemy dishonors both God and others who are "put down" with "killer statements."

It is also why using God to justify murder, terrorism, injustice, deceit and other kinds of sins is a blasphemy against God as well as being self destructive. A daily, specific awareness of the holy, the sacred, the loving presence of God in the midst of the secular world is the road to reverence and all the good things that flow from that.

1. Why is the name of God holy?

"Among all the words of Revelation, there is one which is unique: the revealed name of God. God confides his name to those who believe in him; he reveals himself to them in his personal mystery. The gift of a name belongs to the order of trust and intimacy. 'The Lord's name is holy.' For this reason man must not abuse it. He must keep it in mind in silent, loving adoration. He will not introduce it into his own speech except to bless, praise, and glorify it."[81] *Catechism, 2143*

2. What is blasphemy?

"It consists in uttering against God—inwardly or outwardly—words of hatred, reproach, or defiance.... The prohibition of blasphemy extends to language against Christ's Church, the saints, and sacred things. It is also blasphemous to make use of God's name to cover up criminal practices, to reduce peoples to servitude, to torture persons or put them to death." *Catechism, 2148*

3. What is sacred about our Christian names?

"In Baptism, the Lord's name sanctifies man, and the Christian receives his name in the Church...."

"God calls each one by name.[82] Everyone's name is sacred. The name is the icon of the person. It demands respect as a sign of the dignity of the one who bears it." *Catechism, 2156, 2158*

C. *As Catholics We Believe...*

While it is true there is much beauty in secular wisdom, we affirm that all truth and blessings are gifts of God. Experts appear to explain everything about our surface reality, yet we understand our lives less and less. In our culture everything seems possible, yet nothing is certain. Our outer world goes its way. But our inner selves have lives of their own. We need the depth of faith in God's loving presence and action to nourish the hungers of our souls.

We take three meals a day for our bodies. We must also pray at least three times a day to feed our souls. Psychology teaches us to be self aware. And that is good. But religion takes us further. Faith teaches us to be God-aware. And that is even better because consciousness of God's sacred presence is the heart of the matter about who we really are.

Reflection

Gordon Gaskill has described a pilgrimage he made to climb Mount Sinai. On the morning of the climb, he heard the bell of St. Catherine's monastery pealing, 33 times, one for each year of Christ's life. The bell awoke people of three different faiths. Jewish hikers climbed out of their sleeping bags. Christian pilgrims made coffee. The Moslem guide touched his head to the ground for his morning prayer. Gaskill said that no other spot on earth so justifies the phrase, "out of this world." He had an experience of the sacred which is both out of this world and as close to life as cloth next to our skins.

In My Life

1. What are some occasions in my life when I thought I was not treated with respect? What events can I recall in which I failed to show respect for others? How can I say there is something sacred about me that I don't want others to tread on?

2. How many times each day do I stop and reflect on the truth of God's presence in my heart, in the people I meet and the creation in which I live? How could I improve my awareness of the divine presence and my reverence for the divine name? How does my reverence for God overflow in reverence for others and self?

3. If cursing, using God's name, or blasphemy is a problem in my life, what will I do to stop it? If I am using God to justify sinful behavior, what steps will I take to eliminate this? What can be done to clean up language in our culture, in the movies, on TV, on radio, in magazines and newspapers.

"For the temple of God, which you are, is holy"

I Cor 3:17

Prayer

Holy God, I praise your holy name. I pledge to speak your name only with reverence. I ask the grace to speak all names of all peoples with respect. I beg you to rescue me from using your name to cover up my sins and transgressions.

Glossary

Second Commandment—"You shall not take the name of the LORD, your God, in vain." *Dt 5:11*

Chapter 26

Worthy is the Lamb to Receive Honor, Glory and Blessing

The Third Commandment
"Worthy are you, Lord our God, to receive glory and honor and power...."

Revelation 4:11

Seeking Solace In The Mass

For many baby-boom generation Catholics like Catherine Dillon, childhood memories of going to Mass are as vivid as the powder-blue cover on the *Baltimore Catechism.* She will never forget how her mother seemed transfixed at the consecration of the bread and

wine. ("She didn't even blink.") And she can hear it as if it were yesterday the words of her father, when any of his children expressed doubts about getting out of bed for morning Mass. ("There are people who live where they're not allowed to worship. You should consider yourself fortunate.") They did. Still do. For Dillon, 39, the celebration of the Mass remains the center of her spiritual life. "It gives a sense of calm to my day, to my week," she says. "There can be ups and downs in all other aspects of my life, but Mass is one of the constants." Yet one of the lessons her parents passed onto her was that a spiritual life also had to have a practical side. For her parents that meant participating in the Birthright movement—opening their home to pregnant teen-agers for a few weeks or several months until their children were born. For Dillon, it has meant tutoring a grade school student in religion for the past five years and working in a soup kitchen at Blessed Sacrament Church on Manhattan's West Side. Dillon takes her religion seriously, but she has no illusions about her place in the crowd. "I'm normal," she says proudly. "An average practicing Catholic. A sinner like all the rest."

(Story written by Jerry Buckley, U.S. News and World Report, *April 4, 1994, page 51)*

Do I go to Mass to get something out of it or put something into it?

A. *Some say...*

What can be a more reasonable expectation than to get some payback from going to Mass? Why else go to Mass if we do not get something out of it? After all, the Church teaches that the celebration of the Eucharist puts us in touch with the summit and source of the Christian life. In the Eucharist is contained the entire treasure of the Church, Jesus Christ himself. Yet many claim that Mass is boring, that they get nothing out of it. They argue that there is no point in attending Eucharist when nothing happens to them. So they stop going to Mass. They hear that Eucharist can be a source of blessings and spiritual uplift for them. They listen to the promises of spiritual development associated with attendance at Eucharist. So they go—encouraged by these expectations—and nothing happens to them. After some disappointments they give up the Mass.

Celebrating the Mass

B. *The Catechism Teaches...*

...that God asks us to keep holy the Christian Sunday by active participation in the Holy Eucharist. The spiritual benefits are proportioned to the active involvement we bring to the Mass.

"Participation in the communal celebration of the Sunday Eucharist is a testimony of belonging and being faithful to Christ and to his Church. The faithful give witness by this to their communion in faith and charity. Together they testify to God's holiness and their hope of salvation. They strengthen one another under the guidance of the Holy Spirit." *Catechism, 2182*

The Christian Sunday is the sabbath day. It has two purposes. First, to express our dependence on God by an act of thanksgiving and worship in active participation in the Holy Eucharist. Second, to rest from our ordinary labors so we can engage in play, family togetherness and peaceful renewal of our bodies, emotions, souls and minds. The Christian Sunday is a day to pray and to play, to joyfully give ourselves to God, to happily "let go" of the strains of weekly life and be refreshed and renewed. This is the biblical teaching about sabbath. Just as God rested on the seventh day after six days of "work" in creating the world, so should we rest. (If we must work on a Sunday, we would be wise to devote our official "day off" to rest and personal renewal.) Just as God made the seventh day/sabbath holy, so we should make it holy by grateful songs and prayers of adoration for the blessings of God. This is best done in the celebration of Eucharist.

1. What is our responsibility regarding the Christian Sunday?

"Jesus rose from the dead on 'the first day of the week.'"[83]

"The celebration of Sunday observes the moral commandment inscribed by nature in the human heart to render to God an outward, visible, public, and regular worship 'as a sign of his universal beneficence to all'"[84]

"The precept of the Church specifies the law of the Lord more precisely: 'On Sundays and other holy days of obligation the faithful are bound to participate in the Mass.'"[85] *Catechism, 2174, 2176, 2180*

2. What is the relation of the Christian Sunday to rest?

"Just as God 'rested on the seventh day from all his work which he had done,'[86] human life has a rhythm of work and rest. The institution of the Lord's Day helps everyone enjoy adequate rest and leisure to cultivate their familial, cultural, social, and religious lives."[87] *Catechism, 2184*

3. What is the significance of the parish for us?

"The parish initiates the Christian people into the ordinary expression of the liturgical life: it gathers them together in this celebration; it teaches Christ's saving doctrine; it practices the charity of the Lord in good works and brotherly love...." *Catechism, 2179*

C. As Catholics We Believe...

Catholics believe that we go to Mass first of all to give ourselves to God. The very giving is the "getting." As St. Francis of Assisi taught, "It is in giving that we receive." All week long we have been "getting something out of God,"—life, liberty, existence, love, possibilities, the blessings of family and friends and civic benefits and nature's abundance, etc. The Father, from whom all blessings flow, has been pouring out a treasury of gifts on each of us. We go to Mass on Sunday to show a little humility and appreciation for this stream of gifts. When we participate in the Eucharist from this perspective, then we always "get something out of Mass." Graces, possibly received without awareness during the week, can now be consciously experienced in the midst of the parish Church, with the power of faith synergized by the worshiping community. I pray and worship not alone, but with others and the priest. Faith flows through the whole Body of Christ at prayer. Giving, however, is the secret. If we go to Mass with the sole purpose of giving love, praise and thanks to God, we will experience all the "getting" that we ever need.

Reflection

On August 10, 1904, Giovanni Roncalli —the future Pope John XXIII —was ordained to the priesthood at the church of Santa Maria in Mone Santo. The next morning he went to the crypt of St. Peter's to celebrate his first Mass. He chose the texts from the Mass of Sts. Peter and Paul. Texts and setting, so close to the tomb of St. Peter, moved him to commit himself totally to the service of Jesus and the Church. He used the very words of St. Peter, "Lord, you know everything. You know that I love you." (Jn 21:17) He wrote about his first Mass in his journal. "I came out of the church as if in a dream. On that day the marble and bronze popes aligned

along the walls of the basilica seemed to look at me from their tombs with a new expression, as if to give me courage and confidence."
(Journal, page 171)

Giovanni Roncalli
(Pope John XXIII)

In My Life

1. In following the Church's counsel to attend Sunday Mass with an attitude of giving praise and thanks to God for blessings received, how would I plan to fulfill that call? What daily practices would help me become aware of my dependence on God and of his abundant graces given to me?

2. In what ways could I be involved in my parish liturgy that would make me a "giver of self" at the celebration? If the parish liturgy needs some enlivening and renewal, what would I suggest and what could I do? What life experiences have I had where I discovered giving is getting?

3. At the end of Mass I hear the priest say, "Go in peace to love and serve the Lord." What kinds of practical Christian service do I perform as a response to that "mission call" from the priest? (It would be helpful for you to re-read the chapter on the Eucharist in connection with this one.)

Prayer

Jesus, Bread of Life, I adore you and thank you for the gift of the celebration of the Eucharist. I know and believe that your death and resurrection are made present there and that I receive your salvation made available by the power of the Holy Spirit through the ministry of the priest. Fill me with a generous heart so I may benefit abundantly from this treasury of grace.

Glossary

Third Commandment—"Take care to keep holy the sabbath day...." *Dt 5:12* We observe the sabbath by: (1) Worshiping God in thanks for the blessings of creation and redemption; (2) Resting and relaxing and renewal of our minds, bodies, emotions, souls.
Sabbath—In the Old Testament, the sabbath is on Saturday. In the New Testament, the Christian Sunday is the new sabbath, marking the Resurrection of Jesus who brought us a new creation in grace.

Chapter 27

Strengthen Family Values

The Fourth Commandment
*"A wise son makes his father glad,
but a foolish son is a grief to his mother."*

Proverbs 10:1

Could You Please
Talk a Little Louder, God?

"...and please bless Mommy and Daddy and Lindy and Debbie and Laury and Frosty and..." The four-year old girl paused. Then with her head cocked toward heaven, she asked, "...and could you please talk a little louder, God?"

This is how Debbie Boone O'Neill, daughter of entertainer Pat Boone, introduces an autobiographical essay about her conversion to Catholicism. Her childhood tale now makes her parents smile and evokes nostalgia for the days when her faith was so simple and direct, the kind she yearns for now in her adult years. She says that throughout her whole life she always expected prayer to be a dialogue with God.

At the same time she insists that her relationship with God had to undergo growth and change. Her whole life should progress physically, emotionally and spiritually. In reviewing the road she traveled, she cites the importance of her family.

As one of Pat Boone's four daughters, she had the unique experience of being a preacher's kid and an entertainer's kid at the same time. Even before her father's career burst into celebrityhood, she remembers an environment of Christian values and influences. Her parents took great care to instill in their children a deep faith in God and a pattern of prayer, worship, Bible study and church attendance. This gave them a moral compass amid the marital storms, financial crises, moral compromises and spiritual doubts accented by the Hollywood lifestyle.

The thread of Christian faith endured and blossomed through all of this. Her parents saw the need for spiritual renewal and they joined the Church on the way. The fire of the Spirit entered their hearts in a new way and became all consuming.

Debbie met Dan O'Neill in 1974. The two of them were each on a spiritual journey that would lead them to Catholicism. Through the influence of Bishop Law (now Cardinal Law), Dan was convinced he should become a Catholic. Debbie joined him in the RCIA program. In 1981 they became Catholics. Dan and Debbie trace the roots of their faith journey to their families who nurtured them and set them on a lifelong religious path. God did the rest.

Which is better, the nuclear family or alternative family styles?

A. *Some say...*
There are numerous instances of single parent families doing quite well. Similar stories can be told about grandparents raising their grandchildren. It would seem that alternative family arrangements of this kind can be beneficial for nurturing children who will grow up to be productive and responsible members of society. Since most single parent families are raised by the mother, and often the real father has disappeared, surrogate male role models must be found both for the son's development as well as the daughter's need to know a trusted and considerate male. In these cases the full psychological, spiritual, religious, educational and financial vision of child raising is addressed.

At the same time there are arrangements which are not morally permissible, such as homosexual parents. Moreover, divorced and remarried couples introduce strains and confusions in the nurturing and education of children both in the faith as well as in other values which are not recommended.

B. *The Catechism Teaches...*
...that the Christian vision of the family includes mother, father and children as the plan of God for family life and its positive impact on society and culture.

"A man and a woman united in marriage, together with their children, form a family. This institution is prior to any recognition by public authority, which has an obligation to recognize it. It should be considered the normal reference point by which the different forms of family relationship are to be evaluated." *Catechism, 2202*

The nuclear family, mother-father-children, is the desired form of family life in God's plan for the world. This family should live in such a way that its members care for each other and take responsibility for the young, the old, the sick, those with disabilities and the poor.

Many families are unable to do this by themselves. Other families should help them. Governments and private social and charitable agencies should be ready to help and stabilize the basic family unit. Civil authority has a serious responsibility to foster family life.

The home, the school, the Church, the business world, the military, the government, law enforcement, the arts all have a stake in mutually defending the integrity of the family unit. The health of one depends on the health of the other. Family life is always a matter of morality, faith and values and this should be remembered by all the institutions of society.

1. What are some responsibilities called for by the fourth commandment?

"The fourth commandment is addressed expressly to children in their relationship to their father and mother, because this relationship is the most universal. It likewise concerns the ties of kinship between members of the extended family. It requires honor, affection, and gratitude toward elders and ancestors. Finally, it extends to the duties of pupils to teachers, employees to employers, subordinates to leaders, citizens to their country, and to those who administer or govern it." *Catechism, 2199*

2. What about grown children and their parents?

"The fourth commandment reminds grown children of their *responsibilities toward their parents*. As much as they can, they must give them material and moral support in their old age and in times of illness, loneliness, or distress." *Catechism, 2218*

3. What are some duties of parents?

"Parents have the first responsibility for the education of their children in the faith, prayer, and all the virtues. They have the duty to provide as far as possible for the physical and spiritual needs of their children."

"Parents should respect and encourage their children's vocations. They should remember and teach that the first calling of the Christian is to follow Jesus." *Catechism, 2252-2253*

C. *As Catholics We Believe...*

The breakdown of family life in the United States, evidenced in a high divorce rate and teen pregnancies is well documented. But we should not conclude that the alternative living arrangements which stem from this fact should be legitimized and accepted as normal.

The Catholic Church faced similar family breakdown and "alternative styles" in the days of the Roman Empire and in her confrontation with the barbarians. Polygamy, divorce, abortion and infanticide were common. Instead of compromising, the Church stubbornly opposed these approaches, especially from the time of her liberation by Constantine in the fourth century when she was in a position to do so. For the next thousand years, the Church insistently pressed for what we call the nuclear family and eventually prevailed. Once again the Church confronts a culture which has regressed to many of the problems encountered in the early centuries. The Church does not change her teaching but tries to convert this culture with dialogue, compassion, charitable endeavor, political action, education, religious witness—all the while holding strongly to the teachings of the natural law, the Ten Commandments and the teachings of Christ.

Reflection

"The political community has a duty to honor the family, to assist it, and to ensure especially:
- *the freedom to establish a family, have children, and bring them up in keeping with the family's own moral and religious convictions;*
- *the protection of the stability of the marriage bond and the institution of the family;...*
- *the protection of security and health, especially with respect to dangers like drugs, pornography, alcoholism, etc. ... "*
Catechism, 2211

In My Life

1. As I look at my own upbringing, what positive values will I take from my home life and practice in my family? Why is obedience and respect an important ingredient of family and social life? It has been said, "He who would learn how to rule must first learn to obey." What guidance would I draw from this wisdom saying?

2. Ideally, how does extended family life (grandparents, children, grandchildren, brothers, sisters, cousins, aunts, uncles) enrich me...and how do I enrich them? While rights are obviously important, why are duties just as valuable?

3. I receive much from my family. What should I be ready to give to my family? What is my attitude toward the sick, elderly and disabled in my family or in the families of others?

"Grandchildren are the crown of old men, and the glory of children is their parentage."

Proverbs 17:6

Prayer

Heavenly Father, bless my father and mother, (my children, my brothers and sisters) and all the members of my extended family. Fill me with love and responsibility in all my family relationships. Show me my duties and rights. May I be as energetic in fulfilling my duties as I am in claiming my rights. May unselfish love guide my every act.

Glossary

Fourth Commandment—"Honor your father and mother...." *Dt 5:16*

Chapter 28

Change the Culture of Death—Affirm Life

The Fifth Commandment
"A soothing tongue is a tree of life...."
Proverbs 15:4

Death Chamber Or Life Sentence?

In Mary Higgins Clark's suspense story, *A Stranger is Watching*, the wife of a prominent journalist is murdered at their suburban home outside New York City. A nineteen-year-old young man is found at the scene of the crime. The circumstances of his presence lead the jury to conclude he is guilty of first-degree murder. The judge gives him the death sentence.

Meanwhile, the journalist tries to rebuild his life and that of his eight-year-old child. A public debate arises about the death penalty for the convicted young man. *The Today Show* invites the journalist to be a guest to promote arguments for the death penalty, in which he now firmly believes. His antagonist, who is against the death penalty, turns out to be a very attractive woman. They become romantically involved despite their disagreement on capital punishment.

The plot thickens as it becomes clear that the imprisoned young man is innocent. The real murderer plans to kidnap the journalist's young son and execute him at the same time the convicted young man will be electrocuted. Here we must draw the curtain on the plot so as not to reveal the fascinating twists and turns as it rushes entertainingly to its conclusion.

For our purposes this portion of the story sets the scene for a discussion of capital punishment. It illustrates the debatable nature of the practice, especially when it may mean an innocent person is executed. John Grisham's novel, *The Chamber*, goes a step further and argues against capital punishment even when the prisoner really is guilty and has left behind him a life that is reprehensible in a number of other ways.

More broadly, these stories indirectly lead us to a reflection on protecting all innocent life from practices such as abortion, terrorism, genocide, infanticide, the ravages of war, euthanasia, assassination— in other words, murder in all its forms.

Are there not fates worse than death?

A. **Some say...**

The Church teaches that death is a transition to another form of life. "Lord, for your faithful people life is changed, not ended... Through the saving death of your Son we rise at your word to the glory of the resurrection." (From the Preface of the Mass for the Dead) Is life imprisonment not a kind of living death, a fate worse than death? Does not the Church hold that, in cases of life threatening illnesses, we do not have to use extraordinary means to stay alive?

Have we not always had the right to self defense, even if it means the death of the one against whom we defend our lives or those of loved ones? While war is to be avoided by every possible means, has not Christian tradition established "just war norms" as well as rules against inhumane treatment of civilians and combatants and prisoners during armed conflict? It would then appear there are fates worse than death and that killing is sometimes justified.

B. **The Catechism Teaches...**

...that every human life is sacred from conception to death and that the murder of a human being is gravely contrary to the dignity of person and the holiness of the Creator.

"Human life is sacred because from its beginning it involves the creative action of God and it remains forever in a special relationship with the Creator, who is its sole end. God alone is the Lord of life from its beginning until its end: no one can under any circumstance claim for himself the right directly to destroy an innocent human being." [88] *Catechism, 2258*

The biblical account of the murder of Abel by Cain reveals the presence of anger, pride, hatred and envy in all of us and the tragic consequences to which it can lead. Human enmity can lead to murder. The deliberate murder of an innocent person contradicts the golden rule, the dignity of the human being and the holiness of God. The law forbidding such an act is universally applicable to each and every person always and everywhere.

Anger and hatred are often the root causes of murder. In the Sermon on the Mount Jesus relates the two. "You have heard that it was said to your ancestors, 'You shall not kill;'... But I say to you, whoever is angry with his brother will be liable to judgment...." *(Mt 5:21-22)* And on the issue of hatred, "You have heard that it was said, 'You shall love your neighbor and hate your enemy.' But I say to you, love your enemies, and pray for those who persecute you....' *(Mt 5:43-44)*

1. How does Jesus interpret the fifth commandment?

"In the Sermon on the Mount, the Lord recalls the commandment, 'You shall not kill,' [89] and adds to it the proscription of anger, hatred, and vengeance. Going further, Christ asks his disciples to turn the other cheek, to love their enemies.[90] He did not defend himself and told Peter to leave his sword in its sheath." [91] *Catechism, 2262*

2. What does the fifth commandment forbid?

"The fifth commandment forbids *direct and intentional killing* as gravely sinful.... Infanticide,[92] fratricide, parricide, and the murder of a spouse are especially grave crimes by reason of the natural bonds which they break."

"Since the first century the Church has affirmed the moral evil of every procured abortion. This teaching has not changed and remains unchangeable."

"Whatever its motives and means, direct euthanasia consists in putting an end to the lives of the handicapped, sick, or dying persons. It is morally unacceptable."

"Suicide is seriously contrary to justice, hope, and charity. It is forbidden by the fifth commandment." *Catechism 2268, 2271, 2277, 2325*

3. What is to be said about war?

"Because of the evils and injustices that accompany all war, the Church insistently urges everyone to prayer and to action so that divine Goodness may free us from the ancient bondage of war." [93]

"'As long as the danger of war persists and there is no international authority with the necessary competence and power, governments cannot be denied the right of lawful self-defense, once all peace efforts have failed.'[94]" *Catechism 2307-2308 (For the Catechism's teaching on "just war" doctrine, cf. 2309)*

C. *As Catholics We Believe...*
In our section on "fates worse than death," we have cited instances which do not come under malicious and direct murder. As to capital punishment, the Catechism acknowledges the rights of legitimate public authority to punish criminals. *(2268-9)* But Pope John Paul II, in his encyclical, *The Gospel of Life*, argues that capital punishment is permissible only in cases of absolute necessity. "In other words, when it would not be possible otherwise to defend society. Today, however, as a result of steady improvements in the organization of the penal system, such cases are very rare if not practically nonexistent." *(56)*

Reflection

Terrible noises ring in the ears of those who follow the path of unlove: the silent scream of an aborted baby, the bloodthirsty yells of war, the moan from death row and the speechless gasps from the death camps.

Heard as well are the harmonies of love that celebrate the victory of life: the birth cry of a new infant, the amen of a believer accepting death and welcoming eternal life, the thank-you of a rescued would-be suicide, the cheers when peace breaks out and the grateful tears of a convict with a permanent stay of execution.

Seen in their utter simplicity, these four words, "You shall not kill," demonstrate humanity's deepest belief in a love that affirms human life, a reality so sacred that even the Son of God chose to experience it with us here on earth.

March for Life *participants*

In My life

1. What are three stories I can share which illustrate my belief in the precious value of human life? What are attitudes I can identify in myself that show how life affirming I am? What examples can I cite from people I know which celebrate the sacredness of life?

2. If I were asked to help someone avoid getting an abortion, what approach would I take? Were I in contact with someone who was contemplating suicide, what would I do? What have I done to assist people to overcome self-destructive behavior regarding drugs and alcohol?

3. As I develop a spiritual life and a philosophy of life based on my faith, what are the non-negotiables which will help me maintain a respect for human life at all times? How can my membership in my family, my parish community and my network of friends help me sustain a love for human life?

"I came so that they might have life and have it more abundantly."

Jn 10:10

Prayer

Father in heaven, you created all that lives and providentially see that life continues in being. In you, I live and move and have my being. I thank you for the gift of my life and pray that I will have the utmost respect for all human life. I ask for the courage to defend human life and to grow in appreciation for the gift of life more and more each day.

Glossary

Fifth Commandment—"You shall not kill." *Dt 5:17* The deliberate murder of an innocent person is gravely contrary to the dignity of the human being, to the golden rule and the holiness of the Creator.

Abortion—Human life must be respected and protected absolutely from the moment of conception. Direct abortion is gravely contrary to the moral law.

Euthanasia—Direct euthanasia consists in putting to death the sick, dying and those with disabilities. It is morally unacceptable.

Suicide—Suicide is seriously contrary to justice, hope and love. It is morally wrong. Grave psychological disturbances, anguish, fear of suffering or torture can diminish the responsibility of the one committing suicide.

Chapter 29

With This Ring,
I Thee Wed...Forever

The Sixth Commandment

"The two of them become one body..."
"God blessed them, saying,
'Be fertile and multiply....'"
Genesis 2:24; 1:28

Alexander Attempted to Rape an Eleven-Year-Old Girl

St. Maria Goretti

In 1890, Maria Goretti was born to her parents, Luigi and Assunta. One of six children, Maria was a cheerful and prayerful child. The Goretti's were poor—and made even more needy when Luigi died leaving his widow to raise the children.

On an oppressively hot July afternoon in 1902, eleven-year-old Maria was sitting at the top of the stairs of her home, mending a shirt. No one was home. Then an eighteen-year-old young man, a neighbor, came into the Goretti house, saw Maria and went up to her. He asked her to go with him into one of the bedrooms. She refused. He grabbed her, pulled her into a bedroom and shut the door. He tried to rape her.

Maria fought him, tried to cry for help but he was strangling her so her screams could not be heard. Still, she told him she would die rather than submit to him. In fury and rage, Alexander tore her dress from her body, took out a knife and began stabbing her. As she sank to the floor, he plunged the knife into her back and fled.

Maria was taken to the hospital where she lived for one more day. She expressed concern for her mother and family and publicly forgave her attacker. She died soon after receiving the Anointing of the Sick and the Holy Eucharist.

The court sentenced Alexander to thirty years in prison. For many years he was unrepentant and bitter. Then one night he had a dream in which Maria Goretti appeared to him, gathering flowers and offering them to him. It was a conversion experience for him. He became a model prisoner and was released three years before his term was to end.

Interest in Maria's story grew and miracles were attributed to her intercession. Pope Pius XII beatified her in 1947. After the ceremony, Maria's 82-year-old mother appeared on the balcony of St. Peter's with the pope. In 1950 the pope declared Maria Goretti a saint. Alexander was still alive.

The pope asked young people to be motivated by Maria's example to practice the Christian virtues of courage, holiness and purity, however difficult and hazardous that course may be. Not all people are called to a martyr's death. But everyone is expected to pursue the practice of Christian virtues.

Is the sixth commandment about sex or fidelity?

A. *Some say...*
The very fact it says, "You shall not commit adultery," shows that its main concern is sins of sex. Certainly traditional lessons associated with this commandment have dwelt on the sex sins forbidden by the commandment, such as fornication, adultery, masturbation, rape, homosexuality and divorce. Now with the advances in reproductive technologies, other sins such as artificial contraception and in vitro fertilization (test tube babies) have been added to the list.

Given the sexual permissiveness in our culture, it seems that the commandment's relevance is greater than ever. The loss of classical discipline of our sexual drives is breaking up marriages and families at an alarming rate, is causing a catastrophic rise in teen pregnancies and is witnessing a surge of cases of rape and related violence.

B. *The Catechism Teaches...*
...that sexual activity may occur only within marriage. The bond between unitive (love between spouses) and procreative (begetting and raising children) aspects of marriage may not be separated.

"'The deliberate use of the sexual faculty, for whatever reason, outside of marriage is essentially contrary to its purpose.'" [95]

"Sexuality is ordered to the conjugal love of man and woman. In marriage the physical intimacy of the spouses becomes a sign and pledge of spiritual communion."

"The spouses' union achieves the twofold end of marriage: the good of the spouses themselves and the transmission of life." *Catechism, 2352, 2360, 2363*

Since sexuality is designed by God for marriage alone, any exercise of sex outside of marriage or the marital act is a form of infidelity— to a spouse, to God's loving care for us, to our own personal integrity. This is why the virtue to which the commandment points is fidelity to spouse, God and self in the use of the sexual gift.

The form this fidelity takes is the virtue of chastity. The Catechism discusses this virtue here in paragraphs 2337-2359. However, since the ninth commandment also treats of chastity over against the sin of lust, we will treat of chastity in that chapter. We also suggest re-reading our chapter on the Sacrament of Marriage. *(For Catechism teaching on divorce Cf. 2382-86)*

The aspect of fidelity that commands our attention here is the permanence of the marriage bond between husband and wife. Pre-marital sex introduces a sense of immoral irresponsibility that weakens one's preparation for faithfulness in our future marriage. Extra-marital sex is a direct act of infidelity and strikes at the heart of the marriage promises.

Further, the Church teaches that within marriage there is an unbreakable bond between its uniting purpose (loving union of spouses) and procreative purpose (begetting and raising children). Artificial contraception seeks to have sex without a baby. In vitro fertilization seeks to have a baby without sex. Both acts break the unitive-procreative bond. *(Cf. Catechism, 2366 and 2373-2379)*

1. What is the teaching about conjugal fidelity and marital fecundity?

"The married couple...give themselves definitively and totally to one another.... The covenant they freely contracted imposes on the spouses the obligation to preserve it as unique and indissoluble."[96]

"Fidelity expresses constancy in keeping one's given word."

"Fecundity is a gift, an *end of marriage*, for conjugal love naturally tends to be fruitful.... 'Each and every marriage act must remain open to the transmission of life.'"[97] *Catechism, 2364, 2365, 2366*

2. What about the regulation of births?

"For just reasons, spouses may wish to space the births of their children. It is their duty to make certain that their desire is not motivated by selfishness but is in conformity with the generosity appropriate to responsible parenthood."

"Periodic continence, that is, the methods of birth regulation based on self-observation and the use of infertile periods, is in conformity with the objective criteria of morality."[98] *Catechism 2368-2370* (On this issue read all of *Catechism 2368-2372* and Pope Paul VI's encyclical *Humanae Vitae.*)

3. What are sins against the sixth commandment?

"Among the sins gravely contrary to chastity are masturbation, fornication, pornography, and homosexual practices."

"Adultery, divorce, polygamy, and free union are grave offenses against the dignity of marriage." *Catechism, 2396, 2400*

C. ***As Catholics We Believe...***
While sexual sins are vivid reminders of what the sixth commandment is against, we should be just as energetic at looking at what virtues the sixth commandment upholds: fidelity in marriage, chastity, the proper role of sex meant for marriage alone, the purposes of marriage (loving union of the spouses and the procreation and education of children), the strength of family life that proceeds from these virtues.

The more the virtues of chastity and fidelity are consciously striven for, with the grace of the Holy Spirit, the richer will married life be and the more wholesome will be the environment of the family for the children. Sin constricts and destroys relationships and the dignity of persons. Virtue expands and breathes the fresh air of joy, creativity and hope into marital and family relationships and assures the dignity of persons will blossom.

Reflection

"The life of this simple girl—I shall concern myself only with the highlights—we can see as worthy of heaven. Even today people can look upon it with admiration and respect. Parents can learn from her story how to raise their God-given children in virtue, courage and holiness. They can learn to train them in the Catholic faith so that, when put to the test, God's grace will support them and they will come through undefeated, unscathed and untarnished."
Pope Pius XII, Homily at Canonization of St. Maria Goretti, Virgin and Martyr (*Liturgy of Hours*, Volume III, page 1524)

In My Life

1. For the sake of discussion, let me imagine I did not know the teaching of the sixth commandment. When confronted with rape, adultery and pornography would I think they are wrong? If so, what would be my reasons? What does the teaching of the sixth commandment add to my considerations?

2. What is the only situation in which sexual acts are permitted? What are the two aspects of marriage that form an unbreakable bond? Why is this teaching important? Why did Jesus insist on the indissolubility of the marriage promises?

3. Why is there so much at stake for family life, stability of culture, care of children and the preservation of spousal love in the proper understanding of sex and marriage? As I re-read the chapter on the Sacrament of Marriage, how does that enrich what I study here about marriage in the sixth commandment?

"What God has joined together, no human being must separate."

Mt 19:6

Prayer

Loving Father you created marriage as a gift for man and woman. In your Son, Jesus, you gave us the sacrament of marriage so that divine love, power and grace might be available for the fulfillment of conjugal love and the procreation and nurturing of children. We praise you for this fundamental gift and ask for graces of fidelity for all married couples as well as graces of parenting in their family responsibilities.

Glossary

Sixth Commandment—"You shall not commit adultery." *Dt 5:18*
Adultery—Sexual act between man and woman in which one of the participants is married.
Fornication—Sexual act between man and woman in which neither of participants is married.
Homosexuality—Sexual act between persons of the same sex.
Artificial Contraception—Prevention of conception by some artificial means such as the birth control pill.
Natural Family Planning—Legitimate regulation of birth under certain conditions. *Cf. Catechism, 2366-2372*

Chapter 30

Don't Steal, Don't Treat People Unjustly

The Seventh Commandment

"The thief must no longer steal, but rather labor, doing honest work with his [own] hands...."
Ephesians 4:28

Amos Called Self-Indulgent Women, "Cows of Bashan."

Born in Tekoa around 750 B.C., Amos was called by God to be the first prophet to preach social justice for the poor. He was a mountain man, happy to make a living as a shepherd and a forester looking

after a grove of sycamore trees. He never dreamed of being a prophet, but once God called him, he faced the task with his rough manners and plain talk.

Amos understood that the earth and its fruits belong to God. The Lord entrusted the farms, forests and seas to human beings for their survival and fulfillment. When some men and women grab so much of this for their pleasure and vanity that others have nothing, this is a form of stealing—and clearly an injustice. Amos saw that injustice was stealing on a grand scale, an offense against the seventh

The Prophet Amos

commandment, a crime against the poor.

He delivered his fiery sermons at the shrine city of Bethel, angrily condemning the self indulgent rich who slept on ivory beds, gorged themselves on lamb and wine, wore expensive perfume, while treating the poor with disdain and ignoring their needs. (Cf *Amos 6:4-6*) He saw that they soothed their consciences by regular attendance at worship and practicing external pieties. He confronted them sternly, "I hate, I spurn your feasts...if you would offer me holocausts, let justice surge like water." (Cf. *Amos 5:21; 23-24)* Amos was not against worship, but opposed to using worship as a substitute for moral living.

Bethel was a rich community, profiting from some successful wars and making money on the backs of the poor. Amos faced a stubborn audience. He did not mind being rude. At a local women's club, he addressed them as "cows of Bashan...." (*Amos* 4:1) He warned both the economic elite and the clergy that their moral decadence would make them too soft and weak to resist the impending assault from Assyria. "Your wife shall be made a harlot in the city, and your sons and daughters shall fall by the sword...." (*Amos* 7:17)

The ruling class dismissed him as a religious crank who spoke with a mountain twang. Spoiled children mocked him in the street. They finally tired of him and ordered Amazaiah, pastor of the royal chapel, to use a spurious charge of treason to exile him from their midst. They heard him no more. But they then experienced exactly the doom he predicted.

Is the Seventh Commandment dealing with stealing or injustice?

Some say...

A. The very words of the commandment, "You shall not steal," evidently mean that a prohibition against stealing is its intent. Here is a moral law that possesses new pertinence in the face of multiple forms of stealing in our society: shoplifting, burglaries, muggings, cheating, embezzlement, pyramid scams, phony investment plans, short changing, etc. Millions are stolen through inside trading on the stock market. Millions more are stolen by overcharging the government for services. The curse of drugs moves the addicts to prey violently on the weak to get money for their fix.

The plague of stealing is turning some homes and communities into armed fortresses. Alarm systems, gate houses, high walls, bullet proof glass, ingenious locks, Doberman watchdogs, private guards are among the many defensive maneuvers taken by people to protect their properties, cars and cash. Pervasive stealing erodes social trust. The seventh commandment is not only against stealing, but also for acquiring the respect for people's possessions and the social contract of trust. Its positive virtue makes for an honest and trusting society.

B. The Catechism Teaches...

...that the seventh commandment promotes respect for property and possessions, the need for trust in society. It also opposes stealing and injustice to the poor and needy.

"The seventh commandment forbids unjustly taking or keeping the goods of one's neighbor and wronging him in any way with respect to his goods. It commands justice and charity in the care of earthly goods and the fruits of men's labor. For the sake of the common good, it requires respect for the universal destination of goods and respect for the right of private property." *Catechism, 2401*

From the beginning of creation, God entrusted the earth and its resources to human beings. God has made humans stewards of the earth's abundance. We should care for the earth, work to make its fruits available and enjoy the outcome of our work. The products of the earth are meant for all human beings. We are permitted to have private property to guarantee freedom from poverty, protection from violence, the promotion of our human dignity. We have the right to meet our basic demands and those over whom we have charge.

However, the right to private property, acquired by our own efforts or through inheritance, does not do away from the original gift of the earth to all human beings. Property owners must recall they are but stewards of creation and should use their good fortune to help others to also achieve the dignity and security that comes from ownership and the ability to take care of themselves and their families. Governments have the responsibility to assure this equity for all citizens.

1. What virtues help us keep the seventh commandment?

"In economic matters, respect for human dignity requires the practice of the virtue of *temperance*, so as to moderate attachment to this world's goods; the practice of the virtue of *justice*, to preserve our neighbor's rights and render him what is his due; and the practice of *solidarity*, in accordance with the golden rule and in keeping with the generosity of the Lord, who 'though he was rich, yet for your sake...became poor that by his poverty, you might become rich.'⁹⁹" *Catechism, 2407*

2. How did the Church's social teachings originate?

"The social doctrine of the Church developed in the nineteenth century when the Gospel encountered modern industrial society with its new structures for the production of consumer goods, its new concept of society, the state and authority, and its new forms of labor and ownership. The development of the doctrine of the Church on economic and social matters attests the permanent value of the Church's teaching at the same time as it attests the true meaning of her Tradition, always living and active."[100] *Catechism, 2421*

3. Why must we love and help the poor?

"St. John Chrysostom vigorously recalls this: 'Not to enable the poor to share in our goods is to steal from them and deprive them of life. The goods we possess are not ours but theirs.' *(Homily on Lazarus 2,5)* The demands of justice must be satisfied first of all; that which is already due in justice is not to be offered as a gift of charity. 'When we attend to the needs of those in want, we give them what is theirs, not ours. More than performing works of mercy, we are paying a debt of justice.'" *(St. Gregory the Great, Pastoral Rule, 3, 21)*

C. *As Catholics We Believe...*

The seventh commandment deals with both the personal and social levels of our relations with one another. When it speaks of stealing it treats of the personal level of taking from another what belongs to him or her. When it speaks of social justice, it addresses the laws, structures and customs of a society which should promote fairness and opportunity for all its members.

We all face both the symptoms and the causes of injustice. Mother Teresa, working with the poorest of the poor, ministers to the symptoms of injustice on a one-to-one basis. The late Dorothy Day addressed the causes of injustice, those structures of law, commerce, business, education, etc., which deprive the poor of a decent standard of living, cause them to stay in the poverty cycle and demean their human dignity. In obedience to the seventh commandment, we should oppose stealing, practice charity and justice and eliminate both the symptoms and causes of injustice.

Reflection

"`Economic activity, especially the activity of a market economy, cannot be conducted in an institutional, juridical or political vacuum. On the contrary, it presupposes sure guarantees of individual freedom and private property, as well

as a stable currency and efficient public services. Hence the principal task of the state is to guarantee this security, so that those who work and produce can enjoy the fruits of their labors and thus feel encouraged to work efficiently and honestly...."[101] Catechism, 2431

In My Life

1. When something has been stolen from me, what was my reaction; how did I feel? What instances of stealing do I know about from my experience and what was the response of those stolen from? When people steal merchandise and food from stores, what happens to the prices? How can a sense of trust be restored to our society?

2. What laws can I cite which appear to be unfair to the poor? What practices of the rich cause the poor to be treated unjustly? What needs to be done to assure social justice for the poor?

3. What acts of generosity have I performed for the poor and needy and hungry? Why is concern for the poor a duty and a privilege for Christians? Even though private property is a right, what is the meaning of the Catechism's teaching that the earth's goods are meant for all people?

"I was hungry and you gave me food, I was thirsty and you gave me drink, a stranger and you welcomed me, naked and you clothed me...."

Mt 25:35-36

Prayer

Creator of the earth and all its goods, we praise you for the gifts of creation that enable us to live, experience human dignity and provide for our families. Give us a concern for the poor, a sense of social justice and the means to establish a trusting society.

Glossary

Seventh Commandment—"You shall not steal." *Dt 5:19*
Social Teachings of Church—The Church's doctrine that deals with peace and justice, peace between nations and justice for the poor.

Chapter 31

Nothing but the Truth, the Whole Truth

The Eighth Commandment
"The truth will set you free."
John 8:32

And Regulus Said, "I Have Given Them My Word."

In the third century B.C., there were two powerful city states—Rome, in Italy and Carthage, across the Mediterranean in North Africa. The two cities engaged in a long war, the one to gain control over the other. Among the Romans was a general named Regulus, of whom it was said that he never broke his word.

It came about that Regulus was captured in a battle and brought as a prisoner to Carthage. Alone in his cell he dreamed of his wife and children and yearned to be free. From reports that came to his cell he realized that the Romans were winning the war.

One day some Carthaginian leaders came to his cell with a deal. "We want peace with Rome. We will free you if you do exactly what we say." "What terms do you propose?" asked Regulus. They replied, "Tell them about the battles you lost. Urge them to make peace. If they won't stop the war, you must promise to come back to your prison." "All right," said Regulus, "I promise to return to this prison if they refuse to make peace."

Back in Rome, loving crowds cheered Regulus. His wife and children hugged and kissed him. The Roman rulers asked him about the war. He told them, "They asked me to persuade you to make peace. There are some difficult battles ahead, but I believe that Rome will win the war. Don't stop now. Tomorrow, I return to Carthage and prison as I promised them I would do." They begged him to stay and suggested sending another man in his place.

"Shall a Roman not keep his word? No, I will return as I promised." He bade his family a tearful farewell. He went bravely back to his cell and certain death.

The story of how Regulus kept his word immortalized him in Roman history.

Do we always
have to tell the truth?

A. Some say...

Many have argued that there are situations where modifying the truth for a higher cause is justifiable. Some have said that telling a lie to save a life is all right. Governments sometimes use propaganda—a term that now implies playing with the facts—to promote public policy. Cover-ups are common and the users do not blush when exposed. Someone has said that "Lying is as American as apple pie."

The Pinocchio story rings true because it reminds us how easily we are tempted to lie. The young wooden marionette, Pinocchio, is asked, "Where did you put the four gold pieces?" Lying, he said, "I lost them," even though he had them in his pocket. At that moment his nose grew four inches longer. Under insistent questioning, he lied more boldly and his nose grew so long he could not turn in the room. Confronted with his lies and his predicament, he told the truth. Then a flock of woodpeckers came and pecked at his nose until it returned to normal.

B. The Catechism Teaches...

...that truthfulness is the best policy for truth makes us free, trusting and loving.

"Man tends by nature toward the truth. He is obliged to honor and bear witness to it: 'It is in accordance with their dignity that all men, because they are persons...are both impelled by their nature and bound by a moral obligation to seek the truth, especially religious truth. They are also bound to adhere to the truth once they come to know it and direct their whole lives in accordance with the demands of truth.'[102]" *Catechism, 2467*

In order to tell the truth, we must be truthful. To be truthful demands that we practice honesty and truth-telling every waking minute of every day. Truth is a virtue—and virtue is only acquired by practice. The deepest part of our nature inclines us to being truthful. This becomes evident when we notice how offended we are when someone lies to us. We expected them to tell us the truth. We also get an insight into our gift of truthfulness when we notice the discomfort in ourselves when we are caught lying. Blushing is mother nature's barometer reminding us to be honest.

Though our better nature inclines us to tell the truth, we also have the effects of original sin within us, so that there are times when we believe it is all right to "get away with something...to tell lies." This is why the virtue of honesty is so important. The virtue helps us tell the truth when the weakness of sin wants to undermine our moral strength.

1. What does the eighth commandment forbid?

"Respect for the reputation and honor of persons forbids all detraction and calumny in word or attitude."

"Lying consists in saying what is false with the intention of deceiving the neighbor who has the right to the truth."

"An offense committed against the truth requires reparation."

"The golden rule helps one discern, in concrete situations, whether or not it would be appropriate to reveal the truth to someone who asks for it." *Catechism, 2507-2510* (For a fuller explanation of the offenses against truth, read *Catechism, 2475-2487.*)

2. What is the obligation of public leaders and the media regarding truth?

"Society has the right to information based on truth, freedom, and justice. One should practice moderation and discipline in the use of the social communications media." *Catechism, 2512*

3. What is the relation of the arts to truth?

"The fine arts, but above all sacred art, 'of their nature are directed toward expressing in some way the infinite beauty of God in works made by human hands. Their dedication to the increase of God's praise and of his glory is more complete, the more exclusively they are devoted to turning men's minds devoutly toward God' (*SC* 122)." *Catechism, 2513*

C. *As Catholics We Believe...*

Those who lie for a presumed greater good are wrong. We may never use a bad means to a good end, for the end does not justify the means. In a good moral act the means must be good and the end must be good. However, there are cases where we should remain silent and not reveal the truth to others such as when its revelation would cause scandal, or it would betray a professional secret, or a confidence, or break the seal of the Sacrament of Reconciliation. (*Cf. Catechism 2488-2492*) But keeping silence in this instance is not the same as telling a lie.

When Jesus stood before Pilate he said, "I came into the world, to testify to the truth." (*Jn 18:37*) Our Christian calling involves witnessing truth to our families, friends and to the culture itself. To do this we must keep "a clear conscience before God." (*Acts 23:1*)

Sometimes this includes the call to martyrdom, which is the supreme witness given to the truth, for martyrs hold onto the truth even until death.

Reflection

"Every good Christian ought to be more ready to give a favorable interpretation to another's statement than to condemn it. But if he cannot do so, let him ask how the other understands it. And if the latter understands it badly, let the former correct him with love. If that does not suffice, let the Christian try all suitable ways to bring the other to a correct interpretation so that he may be saved.'" [103]

Catechism, 2478

In My Life

1. In what situations do I find myself tempted to shave the truth and tell a lie? What stories can I tell from my experiences where lies caused a lot of trouble? How do I feel when someone has lied to me? How do I react when I see stories about government lying or business lies - as when advertising labels are false or when travel agents don't supply promised game tickets to tourists arrived at the stadium gates?

2. What safeguards do I put into my life to make sure I always tell the truth? Throughout my life what have I done to practice the virtue of truth? How did my parents teach me to be truthful?

3. Which stories about truth telling from the lives of saints, heroes and martyrs inspire me? What's the best way for schools to handle cheating on exams? What would I do if someone short changed me?

"Let your 'Yes' mean 'Yes,' and your 'No' mean 'No.'"

Mt 5:37

Prayer

Jesus Christ, living truth, you both told the truth and lived it in every way. Deliver me from the wounds of deception and lies and fill me with the Spirit of truthfulness. Grace me with the gift of honest living so I may be a center of trust for all whom I meet.

Glossary

Eighth Commandment—"You shall not bear dishonest witness against your neighbor." *Dt 5:20*

Detraction—Without an objectively valid reason, we disclose another's faults and failings to those who did not know them.

Calumny—Lying about others, harming their reputation and giving an occasion for false judgments of others.

Perjury—Lie spoken under oath to tell the truth in a courtroom.

Chapter 32

Blessed Are the Pure in Heart

The Ninth Commandment

*"The aim of this instruction is love
from a pure heart...."*

I Timothy 1:5

Susanna Screamed For Help

The thirteenth chapter of the Book of Daniel tells Susanna's story, the tale of a woman who chose to be chaste rather than sin. On hot afternoons, the beautiful, young Susanna went to bathe in a secluded pool in her family garden. Two old judges in the community secretly lusted after her. They discovered their mutual interest in her and conspired to force her to have sex with them when she was alone at the pool.

They came to her and said, "Look," they said, "the garden doors are shut, and so no one can see us; give in to our desire, and lie with us. If you refuse, we will testify against you that you dismissed your maids because a young man was here with you." *(Dn 13: 20-21)* Susanna was trapped. She would suffer physical death if she refused, for the "respectable" judges would accuse her of adultery, whose penalty was stoning. But she would suffer spiritual death if she surrendered to them and sinned. What should prevail? The judges' lust or Susanna's chastity?

God's will was her priority. "It is better for me to fall in your power without guilt than to sin before the Lord." *(Dn 13:23)* Then Susanna screamed for help.

The judges accused her of sinning with a strong young man, who fled and whom they could not restrain. They held a summary trial and their accusations were believed because of their reputation and credibility. They sentenced her to death by stoning. Susanna cried to heaven for justice.

The young prophet Daniel was there, heard her cry and believed her innocence. He sought permission to investigate each judge separately. He asked each one, "Under what tree did you see this happen?" The judges gave contradictory answers. Daniel had exposed them as liars. The crowd praised God for saving Susanna who had trusted in the Lord and preserved her chastity. It was the judges who were stoned to death for their malice and lust.

Is all sexual desire the same as lust?

A. **Some say...**

Many, from time to time, have held that, outside of marriage, every sexual thought and fantasy is automatically lustful and therefore sinful. They quote Jesus in defense of this position. "You have heard it was said, 'You shall not commit adultery.' But I say to you, everyone who looks at a woman with lust has already committed adultery with her in his heart." *(Mt 5:27-28)*

Given the powerful nature of sexual desire, its ability to overwhelm chaste thoughts and behavior, it would seem that any occurrence in thoughts and fantasies must be considered lustful. We know that one of the wounds of original sin is disorder in the passions and emotions. This weakness is certainly manifest in eruptions of anger, surges of jealousy, but most clearly seen in outbursts of sexual passion.

B. **The Catechism Teaches...**

...that the ninth commandment urges the cultivation of the virtue of purity and chastity and opposes the sin of lust.

"The heart is the seat of moral personality...."

"'Pure in heart' refers to those who have attuned their intellects and wills to the demands of God's holiness, chiefly in three areas: charity;[104] chastity or sexual rectitude;[105] love of truth...."

"The ninth commandment warns against lust...." *Catechism, 2517, 2518, 2529*

Chastity refers to purity of heart, mind and imagination. Married people who can have sex must still be chaste in heart, and not merely use and exploit each other. Men and women who have taken vows of celibacy and virginity must also be chaste in heart and abstain from sex. Thirdly, all unmarried people, including widows and widowers should also be chaste. Jesus is our model for chastity. Every baptized person is called to lead a chaste life, each according to his particular state of life.

It has been claimed that chastity is harder to practice today because of the sexual permissiveness of the culture and the thousands of messages about sex in the media. But people of every age have had to deal with interior disorder in the passions. St. Augustine wrote about his own struggles in his *Confessions* and praised God for the grace of purity. "I thought that continence arose from one's own powers, which I did not recognize in myself. I was foolish enough not to know...that no one can be continent unless you grant it. For you would surely have granted it, if my inner groaning had reached your ears and I with firm faith had cast my cares upon you." *(Confessions 6, 11, 20)* Check *Catechism* coverage of chastity in *2348-2359.*

1. How does our baptism help us be chaste?

"Baptism confers on its recipient the grace of purification from all sins. But the baptized must continue to struggle against concupiscence of the flesh and disordered desires. With God's grace he will prevail –by the *virtue* and *gift of chastity*, for chastity lets us love with an upright and undivided heart;
–by *purity of intention* which consists in seeking the true end of man: with simplicity of vision, the baptized person seeks to find and to fulfill God's will in everything;[106]
–by *purity of vision*, external and internal;...
–by *prayer*...." *Catechism, 2520*

2. What is the relation of modesty to chastity?

"Purity requires *modesty*, an integral part of temperance. Modesty protects the intimate center of the person. It means refusing to unveil what should remain hidden. It is ordered to chastity to whose sensitivity it bears witness. It guides how one looks at others and behaves toward them in conformity with the dignity of persons and their solidarity." *Catechism, 2521*

3. What are sins against chastity?

"Among the sins gravely contrary to chastity are masturbation, fornication, pornography and homosexual practices." *Catechism, 2396*

As Catholics We Believe...

Regarding sexual thoughts and desires, the *Catechism* says these must be controlled by "discipline of feelings and imagination; by refusing all complicity in impure thoughts that incline us to turn aside from the path of God's commandments...." *(2520)* In other words the temptations may come, but we should nurture the gift and virtue of chastity which will help us resist them and move instead toward God's will.

Regarding masturbation, the *Catechism* teaches: "To form an equitable judgment about the subject's moral responsibility and to guide pastoral action, one must take into account the affective immaturity, force of acquired habit, conditions of anxiety, or other psychological or social factors that lessen or even extenuate moral culpability." *(2352)*

Reflection

"There is a modesty of the feelings as well as of the body. It protests, for example, against the voyeuristic explorations of the human body in certain advertisements, or against the solicitations of certain media that go too far in the exhibition of intimate things. Modesty inspires a way of life which makes it possible to resist the allurements of fashion and the pressures of prevailing ideologies." Catechism, 2523

In My Life

1. If I were giving a talk to teen-agers on how to remain chaste, what points would I stress? Many in the culture claim that since adolescents are going to be sexually active no matter what we say, we should teach them to use condoms and the birth control pill. What is my Christian moral response to that?

2. Many films and TV shows glorify sex. What can be done to change those who peddle this kind of "entertainment"? In my own life what are three practices that help me cultivate the virtue of purity? Who are some role models of purity whom I admire?

3. What social problems affect our society because lust and a failure to be chaste have overtaken so many? What should the government do about these problems? How does the Church help create a better society by encouraging chastity and purity?

"And this is my prayer: . . . that you may be pure and blameless for the day of Christ . . ."

Phil 1:9-10

Prayer

Holy God, you call us to holiness and purity of heart, mind, imagination and body. We pray for the graces to respond to your call and ask for the gifts of holiness and purity that we may witness your love in the world.

Glossary

Ninth Commandment—"You shall not covet your neighbor's wife." *Dt 5:21*

Chapter 33

Greed Vs. Generosity

The Tenth Commandment
"The love of money is the root of all evils...."
I Timothy 6:10

How A Family Was Almost "Killed" With Kindness

Novelist Irwin Shaw in his story, "Bread Upon the Waters," tells a story of how wealth can corrupt. A history teacher, his wife and three children live comfortably in an old fashioned apartment near Central Park in New York City. One night his daughter brings home an old man whom she rescued from muggers. The family envelops him with care, hot soup and their doctor.

It turns out the man is very rich. Their cozy life charms him. He feels he must repay their kindnesses. Thus begins a series of events whereby he uses his wealth to touch their lives. He asks a promoter of rock stars to take their 19-year-old guitar playing son into the business. Their daughter's boyfriend wants to be a crusading newspaper editor. The rich man finds him such a post in a small town in Georgia. Their tennis playing younger daughter needs a college scholarship. He knows a college president who gives her an athletic scholarship.

The history teacher has a heart attack, so the friend finds him an easier job in a prep school where he is on the board. The wife is a painter and would love to see Paris. No problem. The rich man is flying there in his own jet. "Come along."

In a short time, the rich man has overtaken their lives and upset the delicate balance of their relationships, expectations and values. The musical son becomes involved with a drug addicted pop star. The daughter and son-in-law face murderous opposition from the townspeople they intended to reform. Their younger daughter seduces a professor away from his wife. The history teacher and his wife feel disenchanted at the prep school and their marriage is shaken. The rich man has robbed this good family of its integrity.

At the end of the story the teacher and his wife break the evil spell that trapped them. They disengage themselves from the rich man's control. Slowly and painfully they resolve to rebuild their lives and that of their children.

Is it true
that money is the root of all evil?

A. **Some say...**

Jesus often speaks of the problems of wealth. He says that it would be easier for a camel to go through the eye of a needle than for the rich to get into the kingdom of heaven. When a rich young man comes to him and asks how he could attain eternal life, Jesus tells him to keep the commandments. He says he has always obeyed the commandments.

Then Jesus says that if he wants to be perfect, he should sell all his possessions, give the money to the poor and come follow him. The rich man looked sad when he heard this. He had many possessions and could not let go of them.

Jesus often praises poverty of spirit. When he saw a poor widow put a "mite" in the Temple treasury, he said she had given more to God than the rich. For she had given out of the little she had, while the rich gave from their abundance.

B. **The Catechism Teaches...**

...that we should practice the virtues of poverty of spirit and generosity of heart and that we should give up the "love" of money which is greed and avarice.

"Jesus enjoins his disciples to prefer him to everything and everyone, and bids them 'renounce all that [they have] for his sake and that of the Gospel.'"107

"'Blessed are the poor in spirit.'108 The Beatitudes reveal an order of happiness and grace, of beauty and peace."

"The tenth commandment forbids *greed....*" *Catechism, 2544, 2546, 2536*

Like all the commandments which hold before us a virtue to be attained and a vice to be avoided, the tenth commandment proposes poverty of spirit and a generous heart as virtues to practice, while forbidding greed and avarice as sins to be avoided. The seventh commandment dealt with external issues of the right to property and the need for justice, as well as the sins of stealing and injustice.

This commandment deals with the same issues from an internal point of view. If we have the internal attitude of detachment from riches and generosity of heart, we will not steal or treat people unjustly. If we cultivate the interior virtue of poverty of spirit, we will not be greedy or avaricious. Nor will we nourish an crippling envy of the wealth of others. Hence this commandment cautions us against the two capital sins of envy and greed, internal passions and drives that cause the external sins forbidden by the seventh commandment.

1. What does the tenth commandment forbid?

"The tenth commandment forbids *greed* and the desire to amass earthly goods without limit. It forbids *avarice* arising from a passion for riches and their attendant power. It also forbids the desire to commit injustice by harming our neighbor in his temporal goods...." *Catechism, 2536*

2. What does the tenth commandment recommend?

"All Christ's faithful are to 'direct their affections rightly....'"[109]

"Desire for true happiness frees man from his immoderate attachment to the goods of this world so that he can find his fulfillment in the vision and beatitude of God." *Catechism, 2545, 2548*

3. When does envy become an evil?

"Envy is a capital sin. It refers to the sadness at the sight of another's goods and the immoderate desire to acquire them for oneself, even unjustly. When it wishes grave harm to a neighbor it is a mortal sin...." *Catechism, 2539*

C. *As Catholics We Believe...*

Money in itself is not the root of all evils. It is the "love" of money that is the problem. "The *love* of money is the root of all evils." *(I Tm 6:10;* italics mine*)* This is what greed and avarice mean. Envy also plays a role here. In the film, *Wall Street,* Gordon Gekko gives a shameless talk to the stockholders praising greed. The film captured what many moralists and social commentators saw as a fatal moral weakness of the 1980's. Actually it is a moral problem in every age. The Catechism strongly condemns greed and envy, but emphasizes even more the need to acquire the positive virtues of generosity and poverty of spirit— detachment from wealth and material possessions.

Another lesson implied by this commandment is care for the earth and the environment. Greed pillages the environment. Environmental concerns looks with love and wisdom at the earth's resources and treats them as a gift from God for the good of all peoples. Hence we are morally responsible for the environment.

Reflection

There is an old epitaph that says, "What I gave, I have. What I kept, I lost." The only things we will take with us when we die are those which we gave away. Possessions can tend to make us stingy and cautious. When we have very little to start with, we are more open and sharing. The poor understand each other's needs. The rich move away from the poor and forget how tough life is for them.

Generosity never impoverishes the giver. True generosity is contagious. We catch it from others. In the Old Testament, the widow of Zarepath gave Elijah the last food she had in the house. In gratitude he performed a miracle that supplied her with food for a whole year. In the New Testament, Jesus praised another widow who put her last penny in the temple treasury. These two widows knew what the tenth commandment's call to virtue means. So should we.

St. Vincent De Paul, who dedicated his life to poor children and abandoned infants

In My Life

1. In my experience who are the most generous people I know? St. Vincent De Paul said, "You must love the poor when you help them so they can forgive you for the bread you give them." What did he

mean? In our opening story, "Bread Upon the Waters," why was the rich man's approach wrong?

2. What are the worst examples of greed that I can describe? When have I seen envy destroy relationships and ruin people's lives? How can I tell when I am acting out of motives of envy and greed?

3. What steps have I taken to acquire poverty of spirit and detachment from material goods? How am I helping spread respect for the environment?

"Let your life be free from love of money but be content with what you have...."

Hebrews 13:5

Prayer

Holy Spirit, giver of all the gifts so abundantly made available to us, fill us with a generous heart and poverty of spirit. Grant that we may be open hearted to all people's needs and the proper care of the earth and environment.

Glossary

Tenth Commandment—"You shall not desire your neighbor's house or field ... nor anything that belongs to him." *Dt 5:21*

Chapter 34

Prayer: Bread
for Our Faith Journey

"Hear my prayer, O LORD;
to my cry give ear...."
Psalm 39:13

I Look At Jesus
and Jesus Looks At Me.

In 19th century France, St. John Vianney was the pastor of the church in the little village of Ars. His parishioners often found him sitting in a pew before the Blessed Sacrament. "What are you doing?" they asked. He replied, "I am praying. I look at Jesus and he looks at me."

In 1992, a priest was participating in a recruits' Mass in San Diego. One thousand sailors in basic training had crowded into an auditorium for Sunday liturgy. They sang with window rattling volume and said the prayers with the kind of energy they might put into cheering at a football game. After Communion, the chaplain approached the microphone and said in a commanding voice, "Sit up straight. Put your hands on your knees. Close your eyes. Sink down into the catacomb inside you and listen to Jesus." Celebrants and sailors relaxed into a profound silence and opened themselves to meditative prayer for the next five minutes.

Afterwards, when asked if he did anything else besides the "catacomb exercise," he said, "Yes, I also use 'earthquake.' When the recruits are at parade rest on the drill ground, I ask them to lie down on the earth and close their eyes and listen for the earthquake. Remember we are just above the San Andreas Fault. After a few minutes I direct them to become aware of Jesus and pray."

Catholic convert, Caryll Houselander wrote this about meditative prayer: "There should be, even in the busiest day, a few moments when we can close our eyes and let God possess us. He is always present, always giving us life, always around us and in us, like the air we breathe. There should be moments at least when we become more conscious of his presence, when we become conscious of it as the only reality, the only thing that will last forever." (From her book *This War is Thy Passion,* Sheed and Ward, NY, 1941, page 104)

This portrait, a composite, of St. John Vianney, the celebrated Curé de Ars, was made in the same manner that police authorities sketch a composite of a wanted man from descriptions of witnesses, and much of the photomontage was done by police experts in this type of work. In all his life, the Cure never had a photograph taken or a portrait painted.

Do we pray best when we feel like it?

Some say...

It would seem that our best prayers happen when we are in the mood for them. Certainly when we feel a need or experience a crisis we find it much easier to pray. When we feel a religious emotion then we are likely to pray with fervor. Religious music moves some to pray. Sunrises, mountaintops, ocean expanses—or falling in love—move many others to pray.

Feelings have a lot to do with this approach to prayer. These may be feelings of fear for our health and happiness or emotions of ecstasy associated with nature's glories or a new found love. This attitude assumes that prayer is only real when linked to an emotional state. It also argues that one need not pray when not in the mood. In this view the value of prayer is in proportion to the intensity of feelings one is experiencing. Such people pray only when they feel like it.

The Catechism Teaches...

...that the Father calls us to prayer, the Son models prayer for us and the Spirit both teaches us to pray and prays within us. Moreover we should commit ourselves to "pray without ceasing." *(I Thess 5:17)*

"*God calls man first.* Man may forget his Creator or hide far from his face; he may run after idols or accuse the deity of having abandoned him; yet the living and true God tirelessly calls each person to that mysterious encounter known as prayer."

"It is with this confidence that St. James and St. Paul exhort us to pray *at all times.*"[110] *Catechism, 2567, 2633*

When God created us he gave us a capacity to know and love him. We experience this as a search for God and as a longing for nothing less than the infinite. This passion of ours is not useless. God looks for us even more passionately than we seek him. Prayer is the way we meet God and the way God meets us.

The Catechism outlines seven qualities of prayer as found in the Bible. Each quality is connected to a person who exemplifies it. (1) Abraham witnesses the role of "faith" in prayer. What is faith? "Faith is the assurance of things hoped for, the conviction of things not seen." *(Heb 11:1 RSV Tr.)* Hence prayer fills us with assurance and conviction, traits that give us confidence in God's love and promises.

(2) Moses exemplifies the intercessory character of prayer. We beg favors from God, not because God doesn't know what we need, but because we should become aware of what we need and our dependence on God. (3) David illustrates the quality of repentance and conversion in prayer. He sinned and so do we. He repented and so should we. (4) Elijah tells us about the conversion aspect of prayer. He sought to convert Israel back to God. Our prayer is an act of being converted to God ever more deeply. (5) The psalms are the Book of Praise, reminding us of the joy of the prayer of praise.

(6) Jesus models meditative prayer and "surrender to the will of the Father prayer" as he passed many nights in prayer on the mountain. He also taught us the perfect prayer, the Our Father. (7) Mary witnesses the prayer that focuses on Jesus. These seven qualities of prayer should always permeate our prayer life.

1. What is prayer?

"'Prayer is the raising of one's mind and heart to God or the requesting of good things from God' (St. John Damascene, *De fide orth.* 3.24: PG 94, 1089)."

"God tirelessly calls each person to this mysterious encounter with Himself. Prayer unfolds throughout the whole history of salvation as a reciprocal call between God and man." *Catechism, 2590-2591*

2. What is the greatest Old Testament prayer?

"The Psalms constitute the masterwork of prayer in the Old Testament. They present two inseparable qualities: the personal, and the communal. They extend to all dimensions of history, recalling God's promises already fulfilled and looking for the coming of the Messiah."

"Prayed and fulfilled in Christ, the Psalms are an essential and permanent element of the prayer of the Church." *Catechism, 2596-2597*

3. What does the Holy Spirit do in our prayer?

"The Holy Spirit who teaches the Church and recalls to her all that Jesus said also instructs her in the life of prayer, inspiring new expressions of the same basic forms of prayer: blessing, petition, intercession, thanksgiving, and praise." *Catechism, 2644*

C. *As Catholics We Believe...*

We should not just pray when we feel like it. We ought to pray always. *(cf. I Thess 5:17)* It is not true that the best prayer occurs when we have some ecstatic emotions or other kinds of deep feelings. The best prayer happens when we encounter God with an attitude of love and a humble willingness to do the will of the Father through Jesus in the Spirit.

It is not a good idea to let our moods and whims govern when we pray. It is better to pray every day at fixed times, such as when we arise in the morning or go to bed at night. We should pray before we eat and study and work. It is the discipline of prayer that makes it work. Of course, prayer's value ultimately derives from the graces God gives us. The seven qualities of prayer mentioned in part *B* all are connected with divine graces communicated to us.

We bring ourselves to God's presence in order to be transformed into the traits of divine life, such as a divine love which creates a holiness that did not exist before in our lives. Our job is to get ourselves into God's presence, whether at Mass or in a chapel or in our bedrooms, kitchens, family rooms or boardrooms, etc. Then God does the rest.

Reflection

"Dog-tiredness is such a lovely prayer, really, if only we would recognize it as such. Sometimes, I hear, 'I'm so dog-tired when I get to chapel, I can't pray.' But what does it matter? Our Lord can pray just as well through a dog-tired body as through a well-rested one, better, perhaps. It is the same with pain and suffering of all kinds."

Mother Maribel Wantage

"He prayeth best who loveth best
All things both great and small;
For the dear God who loveth us,
He made and loveth all."

Samuel Taylor Coleridge
(These quotes are from the magazine The Living Pulpit, *July-Sept 1993 pp 30-31, 5000 Independence Ave., Bronx NY 10471 914/758-5219)*

In My Life

1. How often do I pray each day? How much of my prayer is devoted to petition, praise and thanks? Who are people I admire for their ability to pray? What difficulties do I have praying? What should I do about them?

2. How often do I pray the rosary? What would help me pray the rosary with more attention and devotion? How frequently do I pray Morning and Evening Prayer from the Liturgy of the Hours? How could I do that better?

3. What effects should prayer have on my daily life? What should I hope to gain by praying? The Mass is a sacrifice of praise. How could I make the Mass more of a prayer of praise for myself and the Church? What should I do to practice meditation each day?

*Raising one's
heart and mind
to God*

"Rejoice in hope, endure in affliction, persevere in prayer."

Romans 12:12

Prayer

Merciful Father, you have called us all to prayer. Jesus, you have modeled prayer both as surrender to the Father's will as well as its contemplative form when you spent nights in prayer on the mountain. Holy Spirit, you teach us to pray and even pray within us. We ask for the grace to respond to the Father's call, the Son's example and the graces of the Spirit's interior work within us.

Chapter 35

The Seven Petitions of the Our Father

"You received a spirit of adoption, through which we cry, 'Abba, Father!'"
Romans 8:15

I Say
An Our Father Very Slowly Indeed

"What an extraordinary thing it is, the efficiency of prayer! ...It's a mistake to imagine that your prayer won't be answered, unless you've something out of a book, some splendid formula of words, especially devised to meet this emergency. If that were true, I'm afraid I should be in a terribly bad position...

I just do what children have to do before they've learned to read. I tell God what I want quite simply, without any splendid turns of phrase, and somehow he always manages to understand me. For me, prayer means launching out of the heart towards God. It means lifting up one's eyes, quite simply, to heaven, a cry of grateful love, from the crest of joy or the trough of despair. It's a vast supernatural force which opens out my heart and binds me to Jesus...

Sometimes when I'm in such a state of spiritual dryness that I can't find a single thought in my mind that will bring me close to God, I say an Our Father and a Hail Mary very slowly indeed. How they take me out of myself then; what solid satisfaction they give me then! Much more than if I'd hurried through them a hundred times...

My God, you know the only thing I've ever wanted is to love you! I have no ambition for any other glory except that. In my childhood, your love was there waiting for me; as I grew up it was with me; and now it is like a great chasm whose depths are past sounding. Love breeds love; and mine, Jesus, for you, keeps on thrusting out towards you, as if to fill up that chasm which your love has made —but it's no good; mine is something less than a drop of dew lost in an ocean. Love you as you love me? The only way to do that is to come for the loan of your own love; I couldn't content myself with less." (*The Autobiography of St. Therese of Lisieux*, P.J. Kenedy and Sons, NY, 1957 Pages 287-8; 308-9)

*St. Therese
of Lisieux*

Does God prefer that we pray with set words or informally?

A. ***Some say...***
God wants us to pray from our hearts, sincerely and with affection. Now it would seem that the best way to do this is with the spontaneous words that course to our lips. In a conversation with someone we love, we would sound phony if we used formal texts or memorized words. So it is with God. St. Therese herself says that she approached God like a child before he has learned to read. Such a child speaks simply and from the heart.

Hence it would appear that God is more pleased with informal prayer than with set words. We know that repeating pre-set formulas sounds stiff. Moreover, this kind of praying very quickly becomes routine, a buzzing that is disconnected from our hearts. Jesus seems to teach this message in his parable of the Pharisee and the Publican. He disapproves of the Pharisee who stood at the front of the Temple and recited long formal prayers and told God how much he did for him. Jesus approves the Publican who stood in the back of the Temple, spoke quietly and asked God to be "merciful to him a sinner."

B. *The Catechism Teaches...*

...that there are many kinds of prayer, formal and informal, all of which can please God. Above all we have the Our Father, the greatest of all prayers, the one Jesus taught us.

"Jesus teaches his disciples to pray with a purified heart, with lively and persevering faith, with filial boldness. He calls them to vigilance and invites them to present their petitions to God in his name. Jesus Christ himself answers prayers addressed to him." *Catechism, 2621*

Jesus always addressed his prayer to his Father. Mary taught him to pray from his human heart. The liturgy of the Temple and Synagogue taught him to pray in regular daily psalms, hymns and spiritual canticles. But beyond this, his prayer springs from a deeper source, the call from his Father. Christ's prayer is filial. This is what he teaches us in the Our Father. We are to say "Our" Father. Jesus is God's Son by nature. We are God's children by adoption.

There are seven petitions in this prayer. They encompass the whole of the Gospel. (1) Honor the holiness of God's Name by responding to the call to holiness in our lives (2) Work to make God's Kingdom present to one another. (3) Do the Father's will (4) Ask for the daily Bread of God's will, the Eucharist and for the needy. (5) Forgive and be forgiven. (6) Plead for strength in the face of temptation. (7) Beg salvation from evil and sin.

1. Why does Jesus ask us to say "Our" Father?

"When we say 'Our' Father, we are invoking the new covenant in Jesus Christ, communion with the Holy Trinity, and the divine love which spreads through the Church to encompass the world."

"In this Son...we are incorporated and adopted as sons of God." *Catechism, 2801, 2798*

2. What do the seven petitions of the Our Father teach us?

"In the Our Father, the object of the first three petitions is the glory of the Father: the sanctification of his name, the coming of the kingdom, and the fulfillment of his will. The four others present our wants to him: they ask that our lives be nourished, healed of sin, and made victorious in the struggle of good over evil." *Catechism, 2857*

3. Why should we pray, "Lead us not into temptation?"

"When we say, 'lead us not into temptation' we are asking God not to allow us to take the path that leads to sin. This petition implores the Spirit of discernment and strength; it requests the grace of vigilance and final perseverance." *Catechism, 2863* (Read *2857-2865* for a summary of the Catechism's teaching on the Our Father.)

C. *As Catholics We Believe...*
God is pleased with both formal and informal prayer, so long as it comes from our hearts, filled with faith, motivated by love and humbly open to the will of God for us. Every day the universal Church prays the "Liturgy of the Hours," a lengthy formal prayer made up of psalms, hymns, readings and other prayers. Also, each day, the Church offers the liturgy of the Mass. The Liturgy of the Hours prolongs the Eucharist throughout the day and night, so that it flows from the altar and back to the altar. This liturgical prayer praises God and begs for our needs. It should be the model for our prayer life.

In addition there are devotional prayers, such as the rosary and litanies and many similar prayers. These foster our faith and bring us close to God. Thirdly there is meditation in all its forms, a way of listening to God so we can do his will. Lastly, but definitely not the least, there are the childlike prayers each of us say in our daily communion with God.

Reflection

"After we have placed ourselves in the presence of God our Father to adore and to love and to bless him, the Spirit of adoption stirs up in our hearts seven petitions, seven blessings. The first three, more theological, draw us toward the glory of the Father; the last four, as ways toward him, commend our wretchedness to his grace. 'Deep calls to deep.'[111]"

"The first series of petitions carries us toward him, for his own sake: thy name, thy kingdom, thy will!"

"The second series of petitions unfolds with the same movement as certain Eucharistic epicleses [prayers to the Spirit to change bread and wine into the Body and Blood of Christ]: as an offering up of our expectations, that draws down upon itself the eyes of the Father of mercies." Catechism, 2803, 2804, 2805

In My Life

1. How have I generally prayed the Our Father? What have I learned that will help me to pray the Our Father with greater attention, love, faith and humility? How would I apply each of the seven petitions to my personal life?

2. How often do I stop and practice meditative prayer? Why is silent meditative prayer helpful in being more attentive to formal prayer such as the Mass and Liturgy of the Hours? Ideally, how would I approach each person of the Trinity in my meditative prayer?

3. What experiences have I had that spontaneously caused me to pray? Did I pray better as a child than I do now at my age? If the answer is yes, why is that so? What is my prayer like when I invoke Mary, the angels and the saints?

"Lord, teach us to pray just as John taught his disciples."

Lk 11:1

Prayer

Dear Jesus you taught us to pray the Our Father with its seven petitions. Send your Holy Spirit into each of our hearts to stir up the desire to pray, so that we will direct our prayers to the Father and seek the gifts we need for our salvation, happiness and fulfillment.

Chapter 36

O Blest Communion, Fellowship Divine: The Communion of Saints

"Here is a call for the endurance and faith of the saints."
Rev 13:10 (RSV Translation)

The Player of Saints Is The Prodigal Son

Leonardo Defilippis a player of saints

The stage actor, Leonardo Defilippis, a cradle Catholic, did not storm away from the Church. He simply drifted away easily, pulled, first by his friends in high school and college, then by his peers in the theater world.

His reconversion was not sudden and blinding like St. Paul's. As the winds of life blew harder and problems were more than he could handle, he searched for an anchor. He turned to God. He began to pray. He recovered the values of his family. "It was kind of like the prodigal son's situation," he recalled. "You say, 'Hey, why am I eating pigs' food?'"

Born in 1952 in St. Helena, California, he was the oldest of six children. "My dad was a butcher. My mother was a homemaker." He belonged to a solid family that relied on common sense, faith, prayer and concern for each other.

Leonardo got into acting in high school. He majored in English in college and took classes in acting at San Francisco's American Conservatory Theater. During the next six years he worked at the Santa Rosa Repertory theater, the Old Globe in San Diego and the Oregon and Colorado Shakespeare festivals.

"The artistic life can be rather wide and open," he said, which means "that pretty much everything is accepted and acceptable even if it is morally wrong. I was involved in the theater lifestyle, which is very transient. Hollywood is an indication, only on a grander scale. I got caught up in all that. Morally, I had to make a decision which way I was going to go."

He saw how drugs and other kinds of self destructive behavior were ruining the lives of his friends. In Oregon he returned to the Church, joined Our Lady of the Mountains parish and met a woman who shared his interests in art and religion. She directed him in a one-person show called "The Gift of Peace," based verbatim on the first six chapters of Luke's Gospel. This was the first of his seven one-person shows, four of which are lives of saints: "St. Francis: Troubador of God's Peace," "The Confession of St. Augustine," "St. John of the Cross," and "Maxmillian—Saint of Auschwitz." Each production includes movement and music.

He married his wife Patti in 1983. They have five children. He tours America, giving from 60-90 shows a year. "It has brought me to the reality of God's presence. Also the love and presence of the saints. Just by doing one person you get to know him as a friend, a brother." Leonardo Defilippis wants his plays to help his audience "to see into their own lives. It's like a window for them to enter more deeply into their faith, into Catholicism." (Condensed from *Actor of the Apostles*, by Bill Dodds, *Our Sunday Visitor* Paper, 8/21/94, pages 10-11)

Is it only saints who are called to holiness?

Some say...

A. Saints who have written or told us about their faith journeys almost always speak about the great graces they received from God to help them on the path to holiness. Some of them had powerful conversion experiences such as St. Paul on the road to Damascus or St. Augustine listening to the inspiring sermons of St. Ambrose culminating in a mysterious experience of God in a garden asking to pick up the Bible—"Take it! Read it!" Other saints had lower key and more gradual inner calls to the life of holiness, often beginning in childhood. Such is the testimony of St. Catherine of Siena and St. Therese of Lisieux. The impression is given that it was to them God addressed such calls and gave them the graces to respond so heroically. Therefore, it would seem that the call to holiness is a special vocation of those people we call saints.

B. *The Catechism Teaches...*

...that God calls all Christians to holiness. We belong to the communion of the church, of heaven and earth. Some of us are pilgrims on earth. Others have died and are being purified. Still others are in heaven contemplating the full glory of God.

"'All Christians in any state or walk of life are called to the fullness of Christian life and to the perfection of charity.'[112] All are called to holiness...."

"'Being more closely united to Christ, those who dwell in heaven fix the whole Church more firmly in holiness.... [T]hey do not cease to intercede with the Father for us....'[113]" *Catechism, 2013, 956*

Holiness is a life of grace and love. Grace is the work of the Holy Spirit conforming us to Jesus Christ and leading us through him to the Father. The love, which is essentially linked to holiness, encompasses the love of God and neighbor. This love becomes visible in our acts of faith, hope, and love regarding God. It further appears in the many virtues which are characteristic of the Christian life: prudence, moderation, courage, justice, mercy, loyalty, honesty, truthfulness, chastity, fidelity, respect for human life and human dignity, etc.

The riches of the sacraments, the example of the saints in heaven and the Church community of the faithful disciples and pilgrims on earth help us to become holy. Jesus strengthens us by his saving grace and inspiring example. We have the remarkable and unique witness of our Blessed Mother as well as her intercession for us. We also have the prayers of the saints to help us.

1. What are some points related to the call to holiness?

"All are called to holiness: 'Be perfect as your heavenly Father is perfect.'[114] 'In order to reach this perfection the faithful should use the strength dealt out to them by Christ's gift, so that...doing the will of the Father in everything, they may wholeheartedly devote themselves to the glory of God and to the service of their neighbor.'[115]" *Catechism, 2013*

2. How do the saints in heaven help us to become holy?

"The witnesses who have preceded us into the kingdom,[116] especially those whom the Church recognizes as saints, share in the living tradition of prayer by the example of their lives, the transmission of tradition of prayer by the example of their lives, the transmission of their writings, and their prayer today.... Their intercession is the most exalted service to God's plan. We can and should ask them to intercede for us and for the whole world." *Catechism, 2683*

3. What is the "Communion of Saints"?

"We believe in the communion of all the faithful in Christ, those who are pilgrims on earth, the dead who are being purified, and the blessed in heaven, all together forming one Church; and we believe that in this communion, the merciful love of God and his saints is always [attentive] to our prayers." Paul VI, *Credo of the People of God, 30.*

C. *As Catholics We Believe...*

The lives of the saints are vivid examples of how God calls all of us to holiness. In all walks of life there are heroes, heroines and champions who inspire others to strive for perfection in similar callings. So it is with the saints. Their experiences help us see that God wants each of us to embark on the life of charity, holiness, perfection, mercy and all the other virtues. They remind us that none of this is accomplished by our efforts alone, but always because of the Holy Spirit's action within our souls.

Such holiness is not divorced from loving service to our neighbor. Love of God and neighbor are the two great laws of Jesus. Saints have built hospitals and schools, fed the poor and worked in jails, defended the helpless and clothed the naked, sheltered the homeless and worked for peace, conserved cultural heritages and created works of beauty, died to witness Christ's truth and preached Christ's Gospel with warmth and effectiveness. Faith and works go together. That is what our own call to holiness implies. Nothing is better for the world. Nothing is better for our own happiness, salvation and fulfillment.

Reflection

"Faith in God is a filial 'yes' said to God, who tells us something about his own intimate life: 'yes' to things narrated and, at the same time, to him who narrates them. He who proclaims it must not only have faith, but also tenderness and love, and feel himself a little son, admitting: I am not the type who knows everything, who has the last word on everything, who checks everything. Perhaps I am used to arriving at scientific certitude with the most rigorous

laboratory controls; here, on the contrary, I must be satisfied with a certitude, that is not physical, not mathematical, but based on good common sense. And more: Trusting in God, I know I must agree that God may invade, direct and change my life."

Pope John Paul I, *Illustrissimi* Little Brown, NY, 1976, page 30

In My Life

1. What do I feel inside me when I hear that God is calling me to be holy? Who are some people I know whom I would consider to be holy? What lives of saints appeal to me? What misunderstandings of holiness can I cite?

2. What changes would I have to make in my life in order to respond to the call to holiness? How seriously do I appreciate that the life of holiness depends a great deal on the work of the Holy Spirit's graces in me? What can I do to respond more honestly to the Spirit's graces? What connection do I see between holiness and loving service to my neighbor?

3. How would I explain the Communion of Saints to a non-believer? How often do I ask the Blessed Mother and the saints to pray for me? Which saints do I tend to ask in particular to pray for me?

"Greet every saint in Christ Jesus.... All the saints greet you...."

Phil 4:21, 22 (RSV Translation)

Prayer

Loving Father, you call me to holiness, perfection, mercy, love and all the virtues associated with sanctity. Give me the grace to respond to this call which is basic to my human dignity and the only path that leads to the true fulfillment of all I am and all I am meant to become. This I ask through Jesus in the Spirit.

Glossary

Communion of Saints—This is the Community of the Church in heaven and on earth: the disciples and pilgrims on earth, those who have died and are being purified in Purgatory, those in heaven enjoying full communion with Father, Son, Spirit, the Blessed Mother and the angels.

Notes From the Catechism Quotations

1. *Gaudium et Spes* (GS) 18:1; cf. 14:2.
2. Vatican Council I, *Dei Filius* 2: Denzinger-Schönmetzer (DS) 3004; cf. 3026; Vatican Council II, *Dei Verbum* (DV) 6.
3. DV 2; cf. Eph 1:9; 2:18; 2 Pet 1:4.
4. DV 4; cf. 1 Tim 6:14; Titus 2:13.
5. St. Thomas Acquinas, *STh* II-II,2,9; cf. *Dei Filius* 3: DS 3010.
6. DV 9.
7. DV 8:1.
8. DV 9.
9. DV 9.
10. Cf. Lk 24:25-27, 44-46.
11. Origen, Hom. in Lev. 5,5: *Patrologia Graeca* (PG) 12, 454D.
12. Cf. Rom 12:6.
13. Deut. 6:4-5.
14. Mt 11:27.
15. Council of Constantinople II (553): DS 421.
16. Council of Constantinople II: DS 421.
17. The English phrases "of one being" and "one in being" translated the Greek word *homoousios*, which was rendered in Latin by *consubstantialis*.
18. Nicene Creed; cf. DS 150.
19. Nicene Creed; cf. DS 150.
20. Gen 1:1.
21. Cf. Ps 51:12.
22. Cf. Gen 1:3; 2 Cor 4:6.
23. Acts 17:28.
24. St. Augustine, *Confessions* 3,6: PL 32, 688.
25. Cf. Gen 1:26-28.
26. Phil 2:13; cf. 1 Cor 12:6.
27. 1 Cor 13:12.
28. Cf. Gen 2:2.
29. Gen 1:27.
30. GS 12:3.
31. Cf. Mt 10:28; 26:38; Jn 12:27; 2 Macc 6:30.
32. Cf. 1 Cor 6:19-20; 15:44-45.
33. Cf. Gen 2:7, 22.
34. Gen 2:24.
35. Cf. GS 50:1.
36. Cf. Council of Trent (1546): DS 1511.
37. Cf. LG 2.
38. Cf. Isa 49:14-15; 66:13; Ps 131:2-3; Hos 11:1-4; Jer 3:4-19.

39. Cf. GS 13:1.

40. Cf. Lk 11:21-22; Jn 16:11; 1 Jn 3:8.

41. Cf. Jn 13:15; Lk 11:1; Mt 5:11-12.

42. LH, Week 33, Friday, OR.

43. Cf. 1 Jn 4:2-3; 2 Jn 7.

44. GS 22:2.

45. Cf. Eph 2:4-5; 1 Pet 1:3.

46. Mt 28:10; Jn 20:17.

47. Cf. Gal 4:6.

48. St. Basil, De Spiritu Sancto, 15, 36: *Patrologia Graeca* (PG) 132.

49. On the *Gospel of John* 11,11.

50. Cf. DS 291; 294; 427; 442; 503; 571; 1880.

51. LG 57.

52. Cf. LG 52.

53. Lk 1:48; Paul VI, *Marialis cultis* (MC) 56.

54. LG 66.

55. Cf. Paul VI, MC 42; *Sacrosanctum Consilium* (SC) 103.

56. LG 53; cf. St. Augustine, *De virg.* 6: *Patrologia Latina* (PL) 40.399.

57. Paul VI, Discourse, November 21, 1964.

58. Cf. Lk 16:22; 23:43; Mk 16:26; 2 Cor 5:8; Phil 1:23; Heb 9:27; 12:23.

59. 1 Jn 3:2; cf. 1 Cor 13:12; Rev 22:4.

60. 2 Macc 12:46.

61. 1 Jn 3:14-15.

62. Cf. Mt 25:31-46.

63. Paul VI, apostolic constitution, *Divinae consortium naturae: Acta Apostolicae Sedis* (AAS) 63 (1971) 657; cf. RCIA Introduction 1-2.

64. Cf. St. Thomas Acquinas, *STh* III, 65,1.

65. *Roman Missal*, EP I (Roman Canon) 96: *Supplices te rogamus.*

66. Paul VI, *Mystery of Faith*, 66.

67. Cf. Mk 1:15; Lk 15:18.

68. Cf. Council of Florence (1439): DS 1325.

69. Jas 5:15; cf. Council of Trent (1551): DS 1717.

70. Cf. Eph 5:25.

71. GS 48:1.

72. GS 47:1.

73. GS 48:1; 50.

74. Mt 22:36.

75. Mt 22:37-40.

76. Lk 15:11-32.

77. Rom 3:22; cf. 6:3-4.

78. Rom 1:5; 16:26.

79. Cf. Rom 1:18-32.

80. Origen, *Contra Celsum* 2, 40: PG 11, 861.

81. Cf. Zech 2:13; Ps 29:2; 96:2; 113:1-2.

82. Cf. Isa 43:1; Jun 10:3.

83. Cf. Mt 28:1; Mk 16:2; Lk 24:1; Jn 20:1.
84. St. Thomas Acquinas, *STh* II-II, 122,4.
85. Codex Iuris Canonici (CIC), can. 1247.
86. Gen 2:2.
87. Cf. GS 67:3.
88. Congregation for the Doctrine of the Faith (CDF), instruction, *Donum vitae*, intro. 5.
89. Mt 5:21.
90. Cf. Mt 5:22-39; 5:44.
91. Cf. Mt 26:52.
92. Cf. GS 51:3.
93. Cf. GS 81:4.
94. GS 79:4.
95. CDF, *Persona humana* 9.
96. Cf. CIC, can. 1056.
97. HV 11.
98. HV 16.
99. 2 Cor 8:9.
100. Cf. *Centesimus Annus* (CA) 3.
101. CA 48.
102. *Dignitatis humanae* (DH) 2:2.
103. St. Ignatius of Loyola, *Spiritual Exercises*, 22.
104. Cf. 1 Tim 4:3-9; 2 Tim 2:22.
105. Cf. 1 Thess 4:7; Col 3:5; Eph 4:19.
106. Cf. Rom 12:2; Col 1:10.
107. Lk 14:33; cf. Mk 8:35.
108. Mt 5:3.
109. LG 42:3.
110. Cf. Jas 1:5-8; Eph 5:20; Phil 4:6-7; Col 3:16-17; 1 Thess 5:17-18.
111. Ps 42:7.
112. LG 40:2.
113. LG 49; cf. 1 Tim 2:5.
114. Mt 5:48.
115. LG 40:2.
116. Cf. Heb 12:1.